NAKED MAGAZINE'S REAL STORIES

ENCOUNTERS AND ADVENTURES

NAKED MAGAZINE'S REAL STORIES

ENCOUNTERS AND ADVENTURES

A Collection of True Stories
From Our Naked Magazine Readers

THIRD EDITION
VOLUMES 3.2-4.2

A Boner Book by
The Nazca Plains Corporation
Las Vegas, Nevada
2005

ISBN: 1-887895-42-6

Published by,

The Nazca Plains Corporation ®
4640 Paradise Rd, Suite 141
Las Vegas NV 89109-8000

PUBLISHER'S NOTE
This is a work of fiction. Names, characters, places, and inci-dents either are the products of the writer's imagination or are used fictitiously, and any resemblance to actual persons, living or dead, business establishments, events or locales is entirely coincidental.

Editor, Blake Stevens
Art Direction, Robert Steele

For Our Naked Reader's

Introduction

===============

Since the very first issue, the readers of Naked Magazine have sent in their Encounters and Adventures for publication in the magazine. We found some of these stories much too "hot" to publish, but we kept them in the back of the filing cabinet -- until now! We brought them out, dusted them off and here they are totally uncut in their original versions.

If they turn you on, titillate you own fantasies or even get you to take a pen in hand and write down your own experiences, then we have accomplished our mission. We want to hear about your Encounters and Adventures so get them to us:

The Editor
Naked Magazine
4640 Paradise Rd, Suite 141
Las Vgas, NV 89109-8000

Who knows? You might just find it published in Naked Magazine!

We hope you will enjoy these stories again if you first read them with Naked Magazine, and if you are a first time reader, then sit back and enjoy the most hilarious, craziest, and erotic true nudist stories ever!

Robert Steele, Publisher

Contents

============================

NAKED MAGAZINE'S REAL STORIES

ENCOUNTERS AND ADVENTURES

A Collection of True Stories
From Our Naked Magazine Readers

THIRD EDITION
VOLUMES 3.2-4.2

Balcony Showoffs

================

A few years ago when I was in Atlanta, I lived on the top floor of an apartment building and had a large balcony off the living room, which I often used for laying out in the sun. There was an identical apartment building next to mine, with a balcony facing me at the same level about 10 or 15 yards away. Because of the depth of the balconies, the way the buildings were designed, and the fact that the balconies had solid side walls but only slim bars across the front, no one could see what went on in the balcony except from the balcony that directly faced it on the other building.

One sunny summer afternoon I looked out my living room windows and noticed that a guy was soaking up some rays on the balcony across from me. I hadn't seen him before and decided to take a closer look. He appeared to be in his mid- to late-twenties, with a firm and attractive body, but he was certainly no bodybuilder. He was laying on an air mattress wearing one of those ugly boxer-type swimsuits and he had on sunglasses. I didn't have anything else planned for the afternoon and I needed some sun, so I put on a thong (I have sort of a thing for skimpy swimsuits and underwear) and went out to the balcony. I turned the long chaise lounge to face my neighbor and spread out my beach towel. I laid down on my back, propped up the back of the chair a bit, and started to read. Every few pages I'd glance up to see what my neighbor was doing. He didn't appear to be doing anything but laying in the sun.

After about 30 minutes, he got up and went inside. I thought that was the end of it but he came back a few minutes later and sat down on the edge of the air mattress facing me. He didn't do anything but sit there looking in my direction. I decided to up the ante and flipped over onto my stomach, showing my bare butt (which was very firm and tan). Because my feet were facing his direction, I couldn't really watch him to see what his reaction was, but I could tell he hadn't moved. I settled in for some sun and after about five minutes, I noticed him get up and leave. Now I was positive that was the end of it. Nevertheless, I turned my lounge parallel to his balcony so I would have a better view of him just in case he returned.

About 10 minutes later, he reappeared with a towel wrapped around his waist and very warily stepped out onto his balcony. He sat down again on the edge of his air mattress facing me but he kept looking around him and fidgeting as if he was trying to make up his mind about something. I just kept still, laying on my stomach with my bare backside soaking up the sun.

Slowly, he turned his body and stretched out on his stomach with the towel still around him. I tried not to appear to be paying that much attention to him and after about 5 or 10 minutes he slowly let the towel fall away to his sides bit by bit. All he had on was a jockstrap. The tan lines from his stupid boxer swimsuit only caused his startlingly white butt to stand out more than it would have otherwise. And it was a beautiful butt! I didn't give any visual reaction but I was sure enjoying the sight and my fantasies were running wild as I imagined us doing all sorts of things with and to each other. We just laid there with our bare butts exposed to the sun - mine in the thong and his in a jock.

After 30 minutes or so of exhilarating but physically infeasible fantasies, my bladder called me back to reality and demanded relief. I was afraid that if I left he would also leave, so I held off as long as I could but finally my only options were to go in and take a whiz or let it flow right there on the balcony. I figured the latter option would probably turn him off so I reluctantly went into my apartment and relieved myself. I was back in two minutes flat and I was even more relieved to see that he was still there; he didn't appear to have moved. It wasn't until I got settled again that I noticed he had taken off his jock and was totally in the buff, but still laying on his stomach.

I wasn't about to be undone by some guy who wears a boxer swimsuit so I slid off my thong and laid back on the lounge, exposing all there was of me. There wasn't any visible reaction from him except that he never took his eyes off me. I decided to up the ante once again. I took a bottle of suntan lotion, squirted a big glob of it into one hand, and began working it into my arms, chest and stomach. As I slowly worked my way down my body I couldn't help but become somewhat aroused (even though I didn't touch myself "there") and I made no effort to hide it. When I finished, I laid back but a part of me remained rather stiff.

I could see his butt flexing and relaxing. I think he was in the same excited condition I was. I reached down and casually stroked myself a few times and he immediately flipped over onto his back and showed all he had. It didn't take long for us to take care of our mutual rigidity. Afterwards, neither of us made any move to put on any clothes and we stayed in the sun for the better part of the afternoon. Just before he went in, he initiated another session of mutual self-gratification. Then he wrapped the towel around his waist, stood up, and disappeared into his apartment with a wave.

Although we never spoke and never made any effort to contact each other, we laid out naked on our separate balconies nearly every weekend that summer. Even when the sun wasn't out, we would occasionally just sit out there in the nude and entertain each other visually. By the end of the summer, neither of us had any hint of a tan line, and we were golden brown from head to foot - and everywhere in between. That fall, I moved away.

Bill C., Louisville, KY

Bare on the Boat

═══════════════

About 10 years ago, my lover and I were camping at a gay campground in Michigan. We went to spend the day at a nude beach along Lake Michigan. We were behind the sand dunes enjoying the sun with our clothes off. It is a popular area for nude sunbathing and cruising.

We met another nude couple and talked about our hometowns and the nude beach. It was their first time there, so we told them about other places in the area. I had been going to the area for years and now my lover and I had been coming up there together for a couple of years. We decided to go for a swim in the lake. We put our suits on and walked down to the lake. In Michigan, you can be arrested for nudity if you can be seen from the shoreline, so we had to wear our suits.

When we got back down to the beach, we saw a beautiful 36-foot boat anchored about 100 feet off the shore. We went swimming out by the boat. On the bow was a nice looking, hairy chested man with his long legs hanging over the side of the boat. We started asking questions about the boat and he invited us onboard. He took us on a tour of the boat and then we sat and talked for a while more. Then he asked if we wanted to jack-off together! We all whipped out our cocks and stared in disbelief. I told him we were all nudists. He then asked if we wanted to go for a ride on the lake. We jumped at the chance to ride on the boat. One of the other guys swam back to shore and got our towels and things, and off we went.

We sailed out onto the lake a little ways and took our suits off. We then sailed around the lake for awhile and enjoyed being naked, sailing under the blue skies. He then stopped the boat. He just let the boat float there. We all went diving and swimming off the back of the boat. We had a great time playing around and just floating there under the blue skies and warm sun. The water was a little cool out there but it felt good.

Later, all five of us went to the bow and layed there in the sun to warm our bodies up from the cool water. We then started to kiss, lick and caress each others' bodies. When the heat from the sun and everything else started to get to us, we then went up to the helm in the shade under the roof. Then we started all over again! It was great to be on the boat naked for about three hours just enjoying the freedom of no clothes, new friends and the sun. That made it one of the best times we ever had. We hoped to see him again but we never did. We are still friends with the other couple we met. Friends from the campground asked us the next day if we were going out again, because if we were, there was going to be a line waiting for the boat to show up! They all wanted to go! I hope we have a chance to do something like that again. It was one experience I will never forget! It was heaven!

Allan D., Omaha NE

Caged Meat

======================

This happened last year in New Orleans. My lover and I had gone there for a long weekend vacation. One night I went out cruising on my own. I happened upon a bar outside of the French Quarter. This establishment had two floors; the lower bar had a pool table and covered outdoor area. The second floor was a smaller area, definitely more leather-oriented. There were leather restraints hanging from the ceiling, a back room and a jail cell.

After cruising the bar (both floors) I decided I would see if I could attract any attention by stepping into the jail cell. No sooner had I gotten the cell door closed when the bartender began giving me instructions concerning the jail cell rules. If I were to remain there, I had to remove all my clothes and give them to him. What?!? Did he know what he was doing? I asked if it was a joke, to which he replied, "No. You do as I say or get out of the cell." Needless to say I followed his instructions and had no intention of leaving the cell or putting on my clothes.

Even though the cell did not lock, I enjoyed the feeling. I occasionally asked other patrons to get me a beer; I felt that I should not break the spirit of the occasion. Apparently this scene did not happen too often, as a lot of guys walked over to look and touch. I was stunned at what was happening. After too short a time, the bar began to empty out, the bartender ordered me over to the bar, and then gave me a beer. The guy next to me was shocked at what had happened and talked no end about me going naked in the bar!

As you may know, there are no closing times for bars in New Orleans, however the upstairs bar did close. The bartender said he had to clean up and close up the upstairs area but he offered to keep my clothes until he was finished with his shift. The man I was talking to suggested we go downstairs to the patio area and talk some more. So, proud and naked as a man could be, I walked downstairs and out onto the enclosed patio. We must have talked for about an hour, during which time my clothes were brought to me.

It was very wild to be naked in a "public" place and to be stared at. After awhile, the guy I was talking to warmed up to the idea but he wasn't ready to get comfortable and shuck his clothes. I tried to get him more in mood, suggesting we go driving around the neighborhood naked, but I couldn't convince him. Yes, he wanted to go home with me, but I told him we could not.

So that ended my wonderful night in New Orleans. I can't wait to get back and check out the jail once again!

Gary, New York, NY

Damn Bird

===============

I'm a 32-year-old bisexual male, and I've been an avid nudist for 10 years. Only once have I ever been caught off-guard.

I was visiting my cousin and his wife at the Air Force base on Oahu. They had a two-bedroom apartment on base, but since I was not their only visitor, I made my bed on the couch in the living room. I sleep in the nude, and during this vacation I made no exception. On one particularly humid morning, I was having trouble sleeping. Not only was it muggy, but there was a bird in a tree outside the window that just would not shut up! I walked over to the window and tapped. Nothing happened. I opened the front door, and again, nothing happened. Only now the bird sounded louder.

I walked outside, nude, to try and "shoo" the bird away. Still unable to get the bird to leave, I decided to just give up. Walking back toward the door, I heard the shower spray and I thought I should get dressed before I surprised anyone with my nudity ... only I was the one who was surprised when I found that the front door had shut and automatically locked behind me!

I was now standing nude outside on an Air Force base in Hawaii at 5 a.m. I walked around to the side of the building to the bathroom window and peered in - just in time to see my cousin's wife going down on him in the shower. I realized I wasn't going to capture their attention. I also realized I was becoming aroused by the whole scene of events.

My only other option was to head over to the security post, which was about 250 yards from the apartment. I tried willing my erection away as I began to walk down the street. Little beads of sweat were forming in my chest hair, not just from the temperature, but as much from the erotic stimulation of the freedom of nudity.

I could see the guard in the glass box staring at me, as I got closer to the gated entry. I was nervous, but the smile I received from the gorgeous, bald, Black guard was so provocative that I was hard again by the time I reached him.

I told him my situation and as he laughed, he ran his hand through the sweaty hairs on my chest. He called my cousin to confirm I was a guest, gave me his spare shirt to wear back to the apartment, and said that he'd look forward to picking it up later that evening.

Needless to say, the lei I received at the airport didn't compare to the lay I received from the guard!

Todd I., Fresno, CA

Easing Steve

A couple of summers ago, my four-year Navy hitch was up, and I was mustered out in Boston. My previous duty station was San Diego and I was determined to go back there when I got out, so I packed my windowless van for the long drive.

I'd met an adventurous 19-year-old blond named Steve in Boston, and he enthusiastically suggested going along as my trip companion and move to San Diego to be my roommate. I snapped up that offer in a heartbeat - Steve was "The Package": long, straight, platinum blond hair to his shoulders; a 6'2", 175# frame of lean, smooth muscle; slab pecs with jutting nipples; smooth flat stomach and slim hips; high, round buns that resembled two pink balloons held together; and a long, slender dick, with a heart-shaped, purple tip and a sheath of thick foreskin, all set off by a wispy bush and big, hairless egg balls. Overall, an exceptional piece of manhood and too exquisite a work to be covered up. Once in San Diego, I hoped to ease Steve into the naked lifestyle I enjoyed, but it wasn't more than 24 hours into the trip when I knew I had an eager practitioner with me, in the flesh, so to speak.

I'd driven the route before, and knew that driving west during the day was a chore. The noon to afternoon rush hours really slowed the pace, and from 4 p.m. to sundown there was a worsening glare from the setting sun. We decided to drive from 10 p.m. until about noon and to save money, stop at rest stops and sleep in the van and for breaks during the night. It was mid-July, and Steve began the trip in cut-offs, a T-shirt and sandals, and with no AC in the van, he was down to cut-offs alone before we'd even left Boston, and for the rest of the trip, wore little more than that. The first night and morning, we made it almost to Pittsburgh and got some rest, and started again later that night. Then the fun began.

For our second break crossing the Midwest, we pulled into a rest stop that looked completely deserted. The lot was empty and the restroom, set back from the lot, was built up against a thick, wooded area. I was already "easing Steve" into the joys of being naked, and had already chucked the heavy jeans and shirt and had been driving wearing only my Navy boxers and moccasins. I needed a shave, and since the place seemed empty, I headed to the restroom dressed just like that.

When I got inside, there was a guy at the urinal arid two more in the stalls, getting me to wonder how they'd gotten here without cars. (It turned out there was a local road through the woods behind the building and this was a huge cruising spot!) As I shaved, the guy at the stall reached through a hole in the partition and was holding and stroking the dick of the guy at the urinal. A few other guys came in, one by one, and leaned on the wall, watching as I was.

I was done shaving but I didn't want to leave just yet, so I looked down at the puff of chest hair between my nipples and just lathered it up and shaved it off. The guy at the urinal turned toward the partition, and the 7 or 8 guys there seemed to all turn their attention to me (hadn't they ever seen a guy shaving before?) I'd already shaved my face and chest, and it struck me impulsively to drop my boxers and shave my pubes. I dropped them and lathered up - and then Steve walked in!

Though far from physically embarrassed, I was worried about Steve's reaction and the impact it might have on our budding friendship. It was a short-lived worry, as Steve looked at the self-groping guys, then to my lathered pubes, and broke into a huge grin. He'd come in to pee, and stepped up to the urinal, but instead of just unbuttoning his fly, he grabbed the waist button and yanked open all the rest of the buttons in one swift move, and let the cut-offs just drop to the floor. He began to pee and also get an erection (my first glimpse of his most endearing trait!). It turns out he gets aroused when naked in front of an audience - a man after my own heart! I was so mesmerized by his hardening cock that I could only stand there, razor still in hand, and watch. He was completely rigid by the time he was finished peeing, and when he was done, he walked away from his cut-offs and sat on the sink, naked, while I shaved my pubes.

Halfway through, I saw him grab the can of foam and lather up his own small bush. When I was done with mine, Steve stood up and pointed at his foamy crotch and said, "My turn!" I knelt and shaved Steve smooth, with all the groping men agog around us. A few other men walked in during the "festivities," and it was fun examining the classic expressions on their faces! When Steve was smooth, I told him, "Let's get out of here," and pulled up my boxers. Steve just picked his cut-offs up from the ground and carried them, strolling alongside me naked and hard! He got in the van that way and off we went! Needless to say, we made many more late-night stops on the trip, and both of us were naked almost all the time from then on. We had more shaving stops, though none as well-attended as the first, and by the time we reached San Diego, the only hair either of us had left was on the top of our heads!

Today, we're still roommates, and as naked as ever, living in an all-male, clothing-optional apartment house. Steve likes the smooth look so much he had total body electrolysis and I've had my nuts, crotch and buns done. I found that Steve liked the puff of hair between my pecs so that's back, as is my thick bush, but Steve trims it like a topiary in various designs, from a crescent to a horseshoe to a triangle to a donut. We enjoy our naked lifestyle and spend weekends at nude resorts in Palm Springs, hiking nude in the mountains, strolling along nude beaches and yes, even making late night visits to highway restrooms to put on the occasional show. My "easing Steve" campaign turned out to be unnecessary, and it taught me a valuable lesson: You don't "ease" into nakedness, you just take the plunge!

Larry, San Diego, CA

Morning Delivery

=================

I have always enjoyed being nude. It all started with a guy who lived two houses from me when I was six years old. We continued the experience through high school then went our separate ways.

Here's a true story: My newspaper is delivered about five o'clock in the morning. I live on a circle and the man who delivers the paper drives by my house, proceeds down the street and as he completes the circle, his headlights shine directly into my front door. I get up in time to be standing at the front door naked every morning and his headlights shine on me as he completes the circle. I go out to get the paper as he passes my house, making sure he can see me wander outside in the buff. I've been doing this for about two years.

About six months after I started doing this, one Saturday morning he didn't leave me a paper. I called the circulation department at the newspaper office and told them I hadn't gotten my paper that morning. They said they were sorry and would notify the carrier and he would bring me one right away. About an hour later (I was in the shower) my doorbell rang and I went to the door-dripping wet. I opened the door and he came in, apologizing all over the place. I had never seen him up close before. Body to die for, blond hair and nice little mustache. He was wearing cut-offs, a sleeveless knit shirt, sandals and a nice compact bulge in his crotch. I told him it was no problem and that I really appreciated him coming back to bring me the paper. (Actually. I think I must've told this to his crotch - I couldn't keep my eyes off of it!)

I offered him a cup of coffee and he accepted. We went into the kitchen and I poured us coffee and asked if he liked to go naked. He responded by stepping out of his sandals, pulling off his shirt and holding his arms out to the side. "You take over," he said. I had a raging hard-on by then and my hands were trembling as I tugged at the top button of his cut-offs. The zipper went down easily and a thick, six-incher, sticking straight out of a blond tuft of pubic hair, popped out of his cut-offs. I pulled the shorts down to his ankles and held them while he stepped out of them, my eyes at the same level as his dick.

Needless to say, our mutual desire for each other got the best of us and we headed straight for my bedroom. We had a great time doing all the things that two guys do in a situation like this and when he left, I told him to not leave me a paper as often as he liked! I never call the circulation department when I don't get a paper now, which is about three times a month. I just hit the shower and go back to bed after door is unlocked.

But I still greet him as he delivers the paper - still nude and lit in the glow of his headlights! God bless the beautiful paper carriers!

Pascha, Panhandle, FL

Paradise Encounter

================

I feel ecstatic just thinking about being outside by the ocean. Every now and then, my travels take me to a place where that is possible. The encounter I describe here took place in January on Bowman's Beach on the north end of Sanibel Island, Florida. Bowman's Beach has been a haven for naked people of all sexes and persuasions for many years. The freedom to be naked has varied based on topography (which changes the beach periodically) and the tenacity of the county police.

Bowman's Beach is a peninsula with the Gulf of Mexico on one side and a tidal river on the other. Access is via a large parking lot at the south end. The beauty of Bowman's is the fact that it is almost all forested by giant pines and other lush vegetation. The white sand beach runs uninterrupted from the south end to a point about three quarters of the way up, where trees have fallen into the water. From there to the end of the island (almost a mile), anything goes. Near the north end is a wonderful open beach protected by trees on both ends.

There are almost always breezes onshore. Even on the hottest days, the forest provides cooling shade. There are many secluded trails that meander through the woods. The place is heavenly.

I am 50 years old. I love this friendly place. A weekday will see from 12 to 20 like souls enjoying this spot. This day in January was special because I had left my cold home (20 degrees!) in the Chicago area and flown to Ft. Myers, FL. My visit to Bowman's began at about noon. The temperature was about 80 degrees and the breeze was warm.

I took my time threading my way through the woods to the beach. I had shed all my clothes just as I entered the woods. I was careful because I wasn't sure how vigilant I should be. I relaxed when I first came on a naked straight couple. I moved carefully through the woods, careful not to scratch any important part of my anatomy! Ten minutes later I emerged onto the beach. Two naked men were walking beside the water and six or eight others were on towels and blankets.

There was a clothed family further on and two late teens/early 20s kids shelling the beach. Shelling is a very famous pastime on the beaches of Sanibel Island and reportedly some of the best in the world. The family seemed unconcerned with our nakedness, nor we with their clothedness.

I love to walk and I love to do so naked. There are very few public beaches where that is possible. I placed my towel down, folded my clothes on top of it, and placed my water bottle in the shade (it's essential to take liquid because there is no convenient food or water close by). I stood there just drinking in the beauty of this place. The azure blue sky was filled with billowy white clouds. The breeze caused the pine needles to softly hum on one side of me and the steady cadence of the waves splashing up onto the sands was symphonic. I was quickly in a daze - no drug could have gotten me higher.

Something unusual happened next. An attractive guy, maybe 28 or 30, came up to me. As most of us 50-year-olds know, even if our abs are flat and washboard-like, we usually have to do the approaching. He was naked like me and pale like me. He asked me a question: "How far does this beach go?"

That question started a delightful afternoon of walking and talking.

This was Joe's first time at Bowman's; I had been coming for 20 years. He told me that he was a golf pro from Wisconsin who was staying not too far away in his grandfather's mobile home. He had come to Florida for January and February and he planned to get as brown as the locals. I commented that there was absolutely nothing wrong with him. He was 6'3", and maybe 200 well-stacked pounds. Not a bodybuilder, but in good shape. His full head of wispy brown hair was combed and appropriate to the man. His manhood (like mine) was pulled up very tightly. He was a good, tight package that was fun to look at.

He invited me to walk with him to the south to show him where the naked area ended. We did just that. We left our footgear on because the shells and cactus that lurk under the pine needles in the woods can be lethal to the bottoms of feet.

We first walked to the edge of the water and then headed south. A hundred yards along, we encountered our first fallen tree. We carefully threaded our way over and under the tree branches. We climbed onto a shelf of shells and sand and sauntered, just enjoying the afternoon. I walked behind him to watch his tight ass tense as he stepped. Occasionally his butt spread open as he climbed over fallen tree trunks. We talked and speculated on just how far we should go. We carefully avoided one couple of birdwatchers with large clunky shoes by slipping back into the woods.

I told him that in years past it had been possible to drive your car or pickup into the woods. One day I had come upon three buck naked construction workers in their work boots, with white butts and golden brown everywhere else. They were standing around the dropped pickup tailgate, conversing and drinking beer. They offered me a beer and I took it.

Then I told Joe, my golf pro friend, about the time I came along the shell ledge and found nestled in between two over-turned pine stumps a family that the Greek god Apollo would have envied. The guy was an Adonis! He was standing with his hands softly resting on his warm, milk chocolate hips. The black hair and the muscular torso were perfect. Lying before him were two Greek goddesses of perfect proportions watching two sweet brown babies. I vividly remember that this scene was laid out on a gorgeous pieced quilt of multiple colors. I watched for a long time as if this was a painting on the walls of some famous art gallery.

Joe and I did reach the south end of the safe area, which was defined by a large blue trash container. It was clear from the tire marks that this was the turnaround spot for the park rangers in their four-wheel drive all-terrain vehicles. We turned around and made our way back. We could easily have retreated into the ocean at any time. On the way back he insisted he was straight and I didn't push him as we wandered au naturel in this most wonderful place. He is a great new friend. We agreed to meet again, perhaps at his home in Wisconsin.

The shadows were lengthening as we shook hands. He departed to his winter home. I stayed and was the last person off the beach that day. I walked back to the car thinking what a fantastic way to make a new friend - buck-naked and in paradise!

Anonymous, Chicago IL

Primal Weekend

===============

My grandparents own a cabin by a small lake in one of the warmer states. I go to college in that same state, and it's about a four hour drive from my school to the cabin. My grandparents generally live there for part of the winter and go back to our home state for the rest of the year.

Since I started school two years ago, my grandparents gave me a key to the cabin. All they ask is that I keep the place looking neat and, if they're there, to let them know I'm coming. During the past two years, I've only seen them twice out in the cabin, once during a holiday and another time during a weekend. Other than that, they're never there. So be it, I've spent many weekends and school breaks by myself in their cabin.

Years ago, a friend told me he had taken his clothes off during a long road trip. He said, "I was sick of the air conditioner and I thought no one would see me, so I took everything off. It felt so good to feel the breeze all over me."

The first time I went to the cabin, I knew I was going to be alone. My friend's comment kept on repeating itself over and over in my mind: "I took everything off. It felt so good to feel the breeze all over me." I turned off the highway onto an old road. The trees made a canopy and it seemed much later than it was. I got a knot in my throat when I realized I could do it. I could get naked and drive all the way to the cabin. I got very excited and nervous. My mind was going over why I should and why I shouldn't get naked.

I stopped the car, stepped outside to stretch my legs and get fresh air to clear my mind. Outside, the air was almost scorching hot. The crickets were chirping and their sounds were coming from every direction. My mind was racing, making me more nervous than I needed to be. I walked over to a bush and pulled off my shirt. I hung it on the bush and reached down to unzip my shorts. I let my shorts slide down to my ankles. Only my feet were covered. I raised my arms and stretched, taking a deep breath. Then, I put my hands behind my head and in that relaxed position, relieved myself. I smelled the warm air mixed with my own scent and the scent of the country air. I could feel the warm breeze on most of me, but I wanted to feel it all over me. I wanted to feel my feet touch the ground and let no clothing limit any of my body movements. As I thought about stepping out of my shorts and removing my shoes, something came over me and I got nervous. I quickly pulled up my shorts, grabbed my shirt, and got in the car and left.

I cranked my stereo and tried to sing along with it to forget the whole incident, but I couldn't. The feeling of being naked was too attractive to me, besides, who would have seen me? If anybody did see me while I was driving, they would only see my upper body and I was already shirtless. I pulled over to the side of the road, opened my door and removed my shoes and socks. I stepped out and again I got the knot in my throat and the feeling that someone could see me. This time, I didn't let my nerves take over. But I did take my time. I walked around and let my feet feel the ground. I walked toward the car and looked at my reflection in the side mirror. I unzipped my shorts and reached in to touch myself. With my hands already inside my underwear, I pulled down my shorts and underwear slowly, and let my genitals feel the hot breeze. I still had a knot in my throat but I also had excitement building up inside of me. I could feel my heart racing.

24

Throwing the shorts and underwear inside of the open window, I thought about walking around before going back inside the car and driving on. Although this was out in the sticks, I knew there were people driving by occasionally. At any rate, I did walk around and sat for a minute before driving on.

The sun was still up when I got to the cabin. I had about one or two hours of daylight left. I took my things out of the car and put them in the cabin. I left the door unlocked and went outside. I was still naked and enjoying the experience so much, I decided to go around exploring.

My feet were sensitive to rocks and branches, but I was glad to be barefoot. This is the way we were meant to be. I found a small trail and immediately started running it. I ran and ran, following the trail, looping around until I came to a clearing that faced the lake. Across the lake was the cabin! I plunged in and swam across, reaching the other side exhausted, but revitalized. The sun had gone down. I lay in the grass and looked up at the stars. I knew I would not use any clothes all weekend.

The following morning, I woke up before the sun came up. I stepped outside and took a dip in the warm lake water. This time, I swam more slowly, just enjoying the water. The only sounds I heard were the splashes my arms and legs made. While in the lake, I saw the sun come up. It was the most spectacular sight! I cannot describe in words the feelings I felt! I got out of the water and went to the cabin to get some fruit to eat for breakfast. I decided I wanted to eat the fruit up in a tree. I don't know where I got the idea, but I just felt like it. I found a pretty good tree to climb and once on a comfortable branch, I ate my breakfast and felt very satisfied.

The rest of the weekend was relaxing and invigorating. I ran, climbed trees, swam, slept and made loud noises. The whole weekend I spent naked and loved every minute of it!

Brian B., Seattle, WA

Showing It off at the Park

================

For every Naked Carl wanting to see naked guys outside, there is a Nude Texan like me waiting to be seen! I have lived in California for only two years, currently living and working in the East Bay Area, although I consider San Diego my home. One Sunday last summer, I ventured out to Tilden Regional Park near Berkeley for some nude sunbathing and hiking, which I have been doing in Tilden since last December. With the temperature having reached the century mark, I needed to find a spot where a cool breeze was blowing.

I undressed as soon as I was out of sight of the main road, looked at my watch - it was 12:30 in the afternoon - and then explored many of the trails in the park. I knew where I wanted to set up camp since there were only two ways to get there: the trail I would follow and a very steep trail on the other side. Once I got there, I spread out my sheet and laid out my beach towel. My nude sunbathing times allow me to catch up on my reading (such as NAKED MAGAZINE!). After about an hour, a bare-chested man came jogging up to my camp on the steep trail. He saw me, glanced over a couple of times, and stopped. He turned his back to me to look at the view of the Golden Gate Bridge, and in about a minute, another bare-chested man joined him. You can imagine what I was thinking during those few minutes! Neither of them seemed to care about me, but I'm sure they hung around a little longer than they probably would have, "catching their breath," and sneaking the occasional glance at me. I was lying spread-eagle on my back reading, and their glances caused me to get a little excited. I made no attempt to hide my growing erection, but before I got too hard, they continued jogging down on the other side.

Shortly after the two men left, a male female couple came walking up the trail I had used. Neither of them appeared alarmed, but she asked her friend, "Is that Richard?" I responded, "No, it's not. Starts with an R, but not Richard."

They walked on by, after also stopping for a view of the bay below.

A few minutes later, I heard the grinding of an engine in low gear. Before I could even think of doing anything, the four-wheel drive Jeep was at my side. I paid no attention until the driver spoke.

"Excuse me. Have you had any complaints?"
"No," I answered.
"Well, if you do, we'll have to move you along." With that, the park ranger put his Jeep in gear and drove down the steep trail.

After another hour or so, I got up to stretch and get my own view of the beautiful San Francisco Bay. I have been considering jacking off on the Golden Gate Bridge, and the thought of that caused another hard-on. After several minutes just standing there playing with my hard-on, a man came walking up the steep trail, pushing his bicycle alongside. I just stood there looking at the view, casually playing with myself. He walked behind me, got on his bike, and rode down on the other side. I laid down for more reading. Since it was getting to be late afternoon, I positioned myself so I got the full effect of the hot sun shining on my dick and balls.

At 6:30 that evening I decided to head home - a very successful day of being seen, I thought. Of course, I couldn't leave without planting my seed next to the pine trees. I opened my

Vaseline, which had been sitting in the hot sun all day (hot Vaseline on my dick is my favorite way to jack off!) and proceeded to rub it all over my dick and balls. I can masturbate for hours out in the hot sun. I walked around the top of the mountain rubbing the warm, slick Vaseline all over my thighs and chest and jacking off, taking care not to rush these exquisite feelings. I decided to lay back down on my back, close my eyes, and listen to the sounds of the forest as I continued to work myself to an orgasm. Occasionally I would hear what I thought were footsteps, but I never opened my eyes, knowing that it was just pinecones and twigs falling from the trees.

After I came, I cleaned up, got dressed, and walked back towards my car. At the bottom of the hill, parked on the trail about 100 feet from the road, was a Harley-Davidson motorcycle. I looked all around but didn't see anyone. Had those been only twigs and pinecones falling from the trees? I can only dream.

R.K. "Naked Texan", Oakland, CA

Image from Naked Magazine Issue 2.4

Sleepwalker

=================

It had been almost two weeks since the last time I came and my nuts were aching for relief. I was trying to break my record of six weeks but no luck. I awoke around 3:30 a.m. with a raging hard-on. I felt this compulsion to go outside, never mind the fact I was buck naked in bed and the sensation of dry sheets rubbing against my bare skin made me even hornier. I got up, put on only my walking shoes, and headed toward the door. In this neighborhood one can leave their doors open without problems. As if not noticing my lack of covering I stepped outside and just started walking my dick pointing the way.

Half conscious, I brazenly walked directly in the middle of the street hoping someone would pass along the intersection and notice me. I reached the first corner looking around for signs of life in what appeared to be a ghost town. The slight breeze grazed the head of my cock, making it swell even larger ... as if it were sniffing for flesh on which to dine.

I thought I was dreaming. I fantasized about getting caught by the police and giving one a blow job while the other fucked my ass with a frenzy releasing that pent up desire they secretly felt for each other but dared not express. I reached the other corner, still no one. Not even a homeless man hunting for abandoned aluminum cans. I ran through the next street as I slowly realized I really was naked and I wasn't dreaming. Fear gripped my heart but at the same time it was very exciting, sexually and otherwise. I reached the corner near my house. Still excited and feeling more emboldened, I decided to take a seat at the corner of the main street under the streetlight. My dick still ached from being engorged and it was time to relieve the stress of my two-week abstinence. I looked around hoping, just hoping, someone was watching me even from a window. I grabbed my cock and started stroking it slowly at first, enjoying the sensation and heightening heart rate. My strokes got faster and faster. I squirmed around like a nympho having a man for breakfast. I lied down under the light thrusting my hips up in the air, posing for any onlookers. I felt myself reaching the point of no return. My body started quivering with pleasure and I let out a passionate "Ohhhhhhh!!!" as I shot loads and loads of accumulated cum. I laid there for a moment panting with disbelief. I heard a car approaching from the other street.

Something told me to stay there and see what happened but my common sense took control and I got up and dashed back in the house.

Once inside I looked out the window to see who it was ... the police.

That's just one of many true stories.

Qhamal, address withheld

Termite Inspection

==================

I am more of an exhibitionist than a nudist. Though I wear as little clothing as possible most of the time, I really enjoy situations where I am naked and others present are clothed. About a year ago, I had an interesting and exciting experience with this type of exhibitionism.

I owned a large, very old house in a large Texas city. Constructed entirely of wood, it required annual termite inspection. For several years in a row, the extermination company had been sending the same technician to inspect - Darryl. A true Texas "good old boy," he was tall and lanky, with a long Texas drawl. He had a nice runner's build, handsome face, and a great "cookie rake" mustache. I always had found him attractive, but in past years, had already learned of his wife and kids. I did not consider him "available."

On the scheduled morning, I had forgotten that he was coming. When he knocked at the door, I was getting ready for work, and was naked. Knowing it was Darryl, there was no need to fully dress, so I quickly grabbed my favorite pair of shorts. The shorts were red nylon running shorts. I had long ago cut the lining out of them, rendering them nearly see-through. They did not cover much to begin with, but I didn't care. I hurriedly threw them on and went to the door, slightly irritated at having forgotten the appointment.

I opened the door, and Darryl's face registered barely concealed shock. He stumbled through a "Good morning," but I was tickled to see that his gaze was taking in everything displayed in front of him. I have a very muscular body, and I work hard on it, so I enjoy it when someone looks at me that thoroughly. My irritation began to turn to amusement, especially when I realized that Darryl was unable to keep from glancing repeatedly at my cock, which was peeking out from under the skimpy shorts.

He first wanted to look around the outside of the house, along the foundation. I decided to walk along with him in case he found any problems. As we walked, Darryl looked at me more than the house. And still, he seemed to linger his gaze on my peek-a-boo cock, which stirred at the attention. After completing the outside inspection, he said he had to go to his truck to get his overalls and flashlight to go under the house. I decided to wait on the back steps at the crawl space access.

It was early in the morning, but the sun was already hot in this part of Texas. I lounged on the steps, leaning back, propped on my elbows. My legs were comfortably spread, and my cock and balls were free of my too-small shorts. I had my head back and my eyes closed, sunning, when Darryl returned.

He came over and stood in front of me, and again looked me up and down as he chatted idly. And I could see that his glance again lingered on my exposed cock and balls. Since he seemed to be enjoying the view, I spread my legs a little further, and moved my hips forward to a more comfortable position. All the while, I was fighting to keep my cock under control. As I did this, Darryl pulled on his coveralls, but never took his eyes off my crotch.

He completed his inspection under the house fairly quickly. I had turned to face the crawl space access when he went under the house, so that when he now came back out, he crawled directly toward my spread legs and crotch. Again, his eyes remained fixed. As he removed his dusty coveralls, I reached down to scratch my balls in my best redneck fashion, when I suddenly realized that he had probably never seen a grown man with a shaved cock and balls! This only added to my excitement. After a nonchalant tug on my dick, I returned to my lounging position. I assumed he was finished with his work, and I was enjoying myself too much for him to leave yet!

But he anticipated me. He suggested inspecting the large garage that I had at the back of the property, something he had never done before. Was he trying to prolong the moment, as well? It certainly seemed so. I opened the garage and stood in the middle as he walked around looking at the studs. As I stood there, I casually hooked my thumbs inside the waistband of my shorts. This caused them to dip down so low that most of my cock was out of my shorts. As he inspected the beams, he kept darting his eyes my way to see what I was doing.

I had an antique car stored in the garage, and he stopped to look it over. As we stood there talking car talk, I decided to step out of my shorts as casually as possible. He never missed a beat in speaking, though his eyes widened somewhat. I could tell he was surprised, but he was trying hard to pretend it was a normal thing for his clients to undress in front of him, in a garage with the door open, facing a busy street with traffic going by in plain view. We stood there talking like this for several minutes. Then he seemed to get an idea.

Maybe he should check the inside of the house for pests? No charge of course. Wondering what he was up to, I agreed. It only took a moment to find out what his game was. He headed down the driveway for the front door. Not one to give in to a dare I followed. Down the drive, across the front lawn, up the steps and across the wide front pourch to the door, all totally naked and in full view of the neighbors and passing cars at morning rush hour.

What could he say? I had called his bluff.

But he wasn't finished with me yet. He did inspect the inside of the house, with me tagging along to see what was up his sleeve. I noticed that every time we came to a large front picture window, he would stand there talking for a few minutes, leaving me in plain view of the street again. I refused to budge. In fact, I think I might have absentmindedly rocked back and forth on my feet as I spoke with him so that my cock swayed around in front of him. If he wanted me to display myself, I would happily oblige. He did not ever acknowledge my nudity, nor did he remove any of his clothes. And I did not want him to - the thrill was me being naked in a situation that would normally require clothing, without either of us reacting.

Finally, paperwork completed, he had to return to his work. As a final send-off, I walked him to the door and stood on the front porch while he walked down the drive to his truck. He sat in his truck for several moments without moving, as if to see whether I was daring enough to remain where I was.

Eventually he gave up, and with a chuckle, he waved and drove off.

I'm sure he had a story to tell at the office, and I hope he did tell it! Certainly, I now have one to tell! I can't wait for the landscaper to show up ...

J.S.E., Albany, CA

Men's Group

================

My men's group had been meeting for about three years. We had discussed lots of men's issues during that time. The group was made up of five straight guys, one bi and me, the only gay man. Attendance had been down and we needed a new push. One of the straight guys, Chad, suggested that we should be more "native" or primitive. We discussed what that could mean and created some opening and closing rituals with drumming and incorporated things from nature. Then we decided that we should take native like names. So I was to create the naming ritual for the next week's meeting.

We had done sweat lodges together and spent time after meetings sitting in my hot tub, so I knew whatever the ritual, the guys would be cool with it. I felt to be born to a new name it should be done naked as the day we all came into the world. There would be candles, drumming and an atmosphere of brotherly love.

When six of the seven of us were there on the naming ceremony night, I had a rusty red, soft blanket on the floor, the drums, some branches and a bowl of water. The room was lighted by several candles. I invited everyone to remove all of their clothes. Slowly, the six other guys moved to various parts of the large living room and proceeded to take off their shoes, socks and pants. But as if on command, they all stopped at their underwear. Each looked around the room for affirmation that those would come off, too. I, of course, had taken my briefs off, so they each followed suit, one by one.

Gil was the first back to the circle. He was about 5'9" with blond hair, fair skin and a firm runner's body. Gil had great calves and feet. He always walked like an awkward teenage boy despite being in his early 30s. Gil had a great cock that swung as he walked and beneath it were some very ample balls. He was a little excited, but not hard. Chad followed. He liked to show off his big, muscular body. At about six feet, Chad had that beefy, naturally well-built body that dreams were made of. Chad was the first straight guy that I had known who shaved his balls. It looked like he had shaved his dark brown chest hair, too, but it had grown back to a nice, stimulating stubble. Chad gave his dick a yank to make sure he got the most of its shorter, but ample length. The three of us sat cross-legged to wait for the others. This, I realized, put our eyes at a perfect level to watch the others join us in the circle.

Next to the circle was Mark. About 29, he had only been in the men's group a few weeks and had just recently become engaged. Mark seemed to want to have new kind of relationships based on openness with men, but was still hearing those voices that said, "Only queers enjoy hanging out with the guys." I was glad he was there. Step by step, he was seeing that men needed each other in deeper, "feeling" ways, and it wasn't at all about sex. It was about support and dropping our fears of intimacy. As Mark walked to the blanket, all that I could think of was that lucky fiancée of his - all that cock and balls for herself! When it got hard, I'd guess that it must hit over nine inches and as big around as ... well, I'd never know for sure. Mark's balls, my favorite part of a man, were "bull balls." They were beautiful. I wondered if Mark knew how beautiful he was. He had a radiant face and the equipment only given to Gods, I suspect.

Rob was next. He dropped down to a sitting position quickly. He's the one considering himself to be bi, but also thinks he might be gay. He has never done anything with a man, but wants to someday. Rob is 56 years old and is in great shape. He has a natural type body without much exercise or workouts, and he stays trim, but not muscled. Rob, too, has a good-sized cock and balls, but I don't think that he appreciates what he's got to the full extent.

Last to the circle was Dean. I had admired him for years and this was the first time that I had seen him naked. He had the hard, smooth body of a 31-year-old construction worker. His red hair and sparkling eyes were a real turn-on to me. Except for Gil, Dean was the tallest in the group, and his long legs were muscled and tanned to his thigh from wearing cut-offs to work. Dean had a beautiful cock, as most redheads did. It was about the size of mine, six plus hard, but soft it appears smallish. I like it when it's warm and my cock hangs soft almost about as big as it gets hard. Dean has that kind of body that is so smooth that it appears oiled at all times.

Just as we were about to begin, the door swung open and Rick came into the room. Late as usual! He was out of his clothes in a flash and didn't even question what was happening. Rick likes to be naked, as I do, and he has a nice tall, muscular frame with no hair except around his cute little dick and balls. Rick is great to look at and proof that it's not size that makes the man. He's very open and is a Taurus, the sign rumored to be the best lover. The last time we held a sweat lodge, Rick was hard from the start. Tonight he remained soft. I noticed that he sat unselfconsciously with his legs wide apart and open to the world.

We drummed and talked about the process to follow. Everyone felt very comfortable and excited about what was to happen. An important aspect of ritual is the element of surprise, coupled with a little fear of the unknown. One by one, we left the room and the others chose a name for the absent man. When we each returned to the room, the others encircled the namee with their arms around each other's shoulders and announced the new name for the guy in the center. Each time the person in the center beamed with joy, because we chose a name that perfectly suited the individual.

When we had finished all the names, we stood in a circle. Eight beautiful bodies lighted by candlelight. We took turns going around the circle of naked men-our brotherly connection. In ancient times men did this because it showed their greatest trust for one another. "Testimony" and "testicle" come from the same root meaning. This event gave all the men a safe feeling of trust. All fears of "What if I touch another guy?" dissolved. All judgments of big, small, right, wrong faded in this process. We each felt accepted as a man, as a brother. We sat back down on the red blanket to share our final thoughts. All the guys loved the event and we decided that after new members were in the group for three weeks, we would perform the "naming ceremony" for them. We have had the event one more time for two new members.

As we sat talking, I gazed around the circle and enjoyed the diverse bodies in my living room. It is amazing to note that of the men in the group who had children, all had sons, eight of them in total, with no daughters. Men are seldom valued for what they give to the world, and their bodies, especially their cocks, are seen as weapons. Looking at these wonderful men made me start to get semi hard. I noticed that Gil, who sat on my left, was semi-hard, also. We both felt all right with it, it seemed natural. All of the men looked and without saying anything, acknowledged each other as a work of God.

When we finished, no one seemed in a hurry to dress and leave. I think that men, in their hearts, crave such solace from other men.

Leader of the Pack, MI

Rent Party

===================

My buddy Adam and I went to a rent party. In case you've never heard of a rent party, it's a party college students throw to raise rent money. These parties can get quite wild and usually attracts many students.

This was in late September so the weather was still pretty nice. Adam's friend Joe lived in the building and had invited us. It was getting real late, about 1 a.m., and the party was winding down. Quite a few of the students had left to go bar hopping before the bars closed at 2 a.m. Some of the few remaining had paired off in couples (boy/girl) and were making out in other areas of the apartment.

Anyhow, in the living room there were just five guys: me, Adam, Joe and two other guys none of us knew. These two guys were pretty wasted and ready to crash.

I was the designated driver so the evening hadn't been as much fun for me. I love to pull pranks so I got an idea. I asked Adam and Joe if they wanted to have some real fun? They were game, so I walked over to them and quietly told them what I had in mind. "See those two guys over there?" Both boys looked and laughed as it was obvious they were pretty wasted and both were dozing off despite the loud music playing. "Let's load them into the back of Joe's van, and take them out for a ride in the country. " Then," I grinned, "we'll strip them naked and leave them to wake up in some farmer's field in their birthday suits!"

Adam and Joe thought it would be a hoot, since we didn't

know the guys anyway. So being careful to not wake them, we loaded each one into Joe's van. Adam got in front with Joe and I hopped in back with the two victims.

Joe tore out of the driveway. When we got out of town he drove a few miles then turned down an old dirt road. We must have been at least 10 miles from the city. He finally pulled the van over at a desolate spot. There was an open field where round bales of hay stood in the silvery moonlight. By the time we reached our destination I had stripped each boy buck naked and they were none the wiser.

Adam and Joe snickered as we took the first guy and carried him out into the field. We lay him behind a bale of hay so he wasn't immediately visible from the road. Adam and Joe went back to get the other boy. I gently positioned the first boy so he was lying on his stomach with his bare butt up. I asked the guys to position the other guy the same way, on his stomach. They did. The two boys lay side by side. I gently put one boy's arm around the other, and shushed Adam and Joe, who were ready to burst with amusement.

Adam and Joe started back to the van. Adam was whispering something to Joe and both boys laughed. I started back and about halfway there Joe jumped me, knocking me to the ground, grabbing my arms behind my back so I lay pinned with my face in the grass. Adam, my best friend, started undressing me and managed to pull my pants down, then off. Then he yanked my underwear off. He ran to the van as I protested to Joe, "Hey, let me go dude, this isn't funny!" When Adam came back he took my sneakers and socks off, tickling my feet as I protested with muffled laughter at the effect of being tickled.

"You like it", boasted Joe.

There was a rush of adrenaline in my system. I pretended I was angry, but it was exhilarating! When Adam came back, they ripped off my T-shirt, which Adam promptly wrapped around his head like a bandana. "I want him totally nude," joked Adam.

"C'mon guys enough already," I protested, "You've had your fun, now let me go."

Suddenly I found myself over Joe's knee being spanked on my bare butt. In hindsight, it must have been hard to take my protesting seriously because I was laughing and Joe & Adam were right: I was enjoying it! The feel off his bare hand against my bare flesh was intoxicating. I was helpless!

I finally agreed to do whatever they ordered, so with both boys holding my arms they led me back to where the intended victims of my prank lay in blissful sleep.

Adam shoved my face right into one guy's butt and I had to kiss it, then the other boy. I protested, but I was enjoying it and had not put up anything more than a pretend struggle. Then they had me licking their asscheeks with my tongue. Joe and Adam chided me on in humiliation. Suddenly one of the boys started to stir. Joe and Adam ran away lickety split. I was horrified, but the boy fell back into slumber.

It wasn't until I heard the van start up that I realized what was happening. I jumped up and ran toward the road as they sped away, laughing hysterically.

I was the victim of my own prank, left stark naked in the middle of nowhere with two nude dudes I didn't even know! Realizing I couldn't walk the 10 or 12 miles to town in my birthday suit, I decided I'd have to wait until morning to figure a way out of this situation.

I walked back to the other nude dudes. Their bare butts looked so cute in the moonlight. If I only had a couple of condoms, I thought to myself. Because I was getting a little chilly, I used one of the butts for a pillow and I covered myself up with the other guy, sort of like a human blanket.

When we all awoke, around the same time, the sun was shining and a farmer, probably in his 50s, was standing over us laughing good-naturedly. "Fraternity prank?" he grinned. The other two boys were stone silent. They were obviously embarrassed at being caught naked and had terrible hangovers. I nodded yes and smiled meekly.

"Stay here and I'll get you boys some clothes," said the farmer.

"We aren't going anywhere," blurted one of the boys. Then we all laughed.

Name and address withheld

Naked Boating

================

The sun was barely visible as Eric and I launched our little boat on a sandy ramp at the municipal beach on the Intercoastal Waterway about 25 miles south of Daytona Beach. We were headed across the channel into the backwaters to fish for speckled sea trout.

We trolled along the shoreline catching a fish here and there, enough for a meal or two. When it warmed up we took our shirts off followed soon after (as if by mutual consent) by our pants. We weren't worried about anyone seeing us as no one hardly ever went back there and if they did we would hear the noise of their motor and have plenty of time to slip our pants on.

It seemed natural to be nude, moving slowly along the quiet backwaters. We soon gave up fishing and were content to cruise around the mangrove islands heading toward our favorite sandbar for a swim. Beaching the boat, we dove into the cool water and splashed around like little kids. We were both 22 years old, tall and skinny with sun-bleached hair, looking more like brothers than best friends. Fooling around for an hour or so, we laid on the sand talking softly, finishing off the six-pack we had brought with us. After one last dive to rinse the sand off, we set back for home.

Cruising along admiring the scenery, we watched the herons tiptoeing along the water's edge searching for small fish, porpoises playing just yards away, a huge sea turtle coming up for air right in front of the boat! I had just enough time to yell, "Watch out!" before we slid up on the turtle's back, pitching us both into the water and nearly capsizing the boat. Splashing my way to the surface, I looked for Eric. He was treading water about 10 feet away looking bewildered. We were both okay and started to laugh as I told him, "This crap only happens to tourists!" We watched our boat, oblivious of its missing crew; cruise serenely toward a bank of mangroves a hundred yards away. Feeling foolish, we swam toward it.

Climbing back into the boat we were stunned to find it completely empty. We both realized it would be futile searching for anything. The current and water depth would make it impossible. We sat there cursing, thinking of the hassle it would be to replace everything we had lost. When the full impact of our predicament hit us: our clothes were gone!

We had to get back and the only way was the way we were, naked as jaybirds! Starting out again we began nervously giggling and talking about what idiots we were and how embarrassing this was going to be. Rounding the last bend to the main channel, I slowed down and looked across the waterway. I could see people sunning themselves and splashing in the water. Thankfully, it was a weekday and no kids were around. This was the gauntlet we would have to run in our birthday suit.

"Well, are you ready to make a complete ass of yourself?" I questioned Eric.

He gave a little half grin and answered back,

"Why don't we just go ashore like we normally do and just ignore everyone?"

"You can do that," I answered, "I'm going to break the record for the 100-yard dash."

Coming across the channel I was astonished to see Eric's dick getting hard. I hollered over the noise of the motor, "Goddammit Eric, do something about that thing," motioning toward his lengthening rod.

He nodded and shrugged. I watched stupefied as he pushed it down a couple of times and let it spring back and slap against his belly.

"Do something, anything!" I yelled.

"What the fuck do you want me to do, jerk off?" he yelled back sarcastically.

I could see people on the shore starting to look our way and point. I could feel my face begin to blush. It was probably as red as the head of Eric's dick, which was still straining upward. Getting scared, I could feel my cock and balls constrict, trying to hide in my pubic hair while incredulously Eric's was bursting at the seams! I thought to myself that he's going to look like a super stud while I was going to look like a fucking eunuch!

I was feeling more helpless and out of control than ever. If I could have conjured up an iceberg I would have made like the Titanic and gladly gone down with the ship. Eric could see the way I was looking at him, and shrugging his shoulders he hollered, "Maybe it'll go down if I took a cold shower." I wasn't in the mood for humor and wanted to deep-six his ass right there but we were coming to the launch ramp and I knew I was the one that was sinking.

I hadn't realized it at the time but our voices had carried across the water and everyone on the beach had heard our conversation as we approached the shore. They stared at us in utter disbelief as the boat surged onto the sand with an unworldly screech.

We scrambled out and hauled ass to the car, with Eric's stiff pecker pointing the way. I skidded to a halt and bent down, unthinkingly mooning the crowd, searching frantically under the bumper for the magnetic holder that held my spare keys. Eric was hopping around with his dick bobbing up and down hollering, "Get the fucking keys you clumsy shit!" For a god awful second I thought they weren't there but finally found them and tore the box open, racing around and unlocking the car door, then jumping in.

In a moment of madness I thought of humbling Eric and leaving him stranded outside but it swiftly passed and I unlocked his door and let him in. We looked over at the beach and could see most of the crowd practically rolling on the ground laughing -but a few were glaring and I'm sure were hoping lightning would strike us!

Our last dilemma: We still had to get the boat on the trailer or leave it. We were arguing what to do when mercifully two men still laughing came over and asked if we had a problem. "A problem" was an understatement. We explained the situation to them, they said to back the trailer down the ramp, and they would fix us up. I could have kissed them and I thanked them repeatedly. With the boat secured, our audience knew the spectacle was over and started to clap. For a second I thought Eric was going to get out and take a bow but even he thought better of it. If he had, I swear I would have left his naked ass right there but Eric was content to just wave.

Unbelievably, during this whole escapade, Eric's erection never went down and it was still pointing toward the sky as we drove off.

Grabbing his cock, he looked at me sheepishly and asked

"What the fuck was I supposed to do? The goddam thing wouldn't go down"

"Well don't beat it now" I answered,

"I'll take care of that sucker when we get home."

" I was hoping you would say that" Eric replied grinning.
And I did.

Frank B., Edgewater, FL

Total Tan

===============

The summer after my junior year of college, I stayed on campus. These college summers were enjoyable: the campus was quieter; my class schedule was lighter-and the warm California sun felt good on naked skin. I decided to get my first total body tan. I tried sunning in remote outdoor areas, but found them neither comfortable nor particularly interesting. So I placed an ad in an "alternative" paper that was circulated in the surrounding community, seeking a "hassle-free" environment for nude sunbathing. "Total privacy not required, male-oriented preferred."

I rejected most of my replies immediately, but found one that sounded promising. We talked, and I agreed to drop by. I arrived barefoot, wearing only loose gym shorts and a tank top. "Bob" proved to be a very butch man of about 30, a cop, who lived alone. We chatted a bit in his kitchen, from where I could see that his patio was indeed very private. Suddenly he suggested that "I get working on my tan:" and that I could "leave my clothes here." There was silence, and he looked at me. I was surprised-I had imagined that I'd strip on the patio-but the expectation was clear. He didn't avert his eyes as I shucked off my clothes in his kitchen. He commented on my existing tan line-studying the pale skin of my groin carefully-before suggesting that he thought I'd tan well. I felt very much on display, and was both embarrassed and aroused by the attention. Only when I was nude did he offer to show me around. I found this episode to be both arousing and disconcerting-that I was being told to strip naked before I was ready, and that I was vulnerably exposed before a fully clothed man. I began to develop my total tan under his watchful eyes.

The expectation that I'd strip nude in his house upon arrival was established quickly. On my second visit, he greeted me in the entry hall with, "Let me take your clothes." I stripped, and was mildly disconcerted when he disappeared with them into the back of his house. But I found the combination of being naked and without any control of my clothes exciting.

After a few sessions, he invited me to use his backyard on afternoons when he was working. If I left him a message, he'd leave the gate on the far side of his garage unlocked so I could enter through the side yard. I loved this! As soon as I entered his yard, I'd strip, leaving my clothes beside the gate, and explore his backyard nude. The combination of nudity, sun, and college jock hormones resulted in routine prolonged J/ O sessions on his patio. After several days of this, I was surprised to find his car in the driveway when I left. I felt the hood - it was cool, which meant he had been home for a while. He probably saw me jack off! I wondered if I had overstepped my boundaries - would he want me to return?

A few days later, the answer arrived: he left a message that he was leaving the gate unlocked on a date that he knew I had no afternoon classes, "in case I wanted to tan."

Of course I did. He didn't seem to be home, so I stripped as usual, jerked off, and dozed in the sun. But again I found his car in the driveway when I left. This became routine: I found that if I told him the approximate time I'd be at his house, I'd usually find evidence upon leaving that he had been there to watch.

Then one day, he came out on the patio after my ejaculation. There was no hiding the evidence-I was still hard, and there was obvious cum on my chest and belly-but we didn't speak about that. Nevertheless, we both understood that he had watched me; another threshold had been broken.

The process of increasing the ante began. When I was ready to leave, he escorted me into the house, naked, and to the front door. I remarked that my shorts were in the side yard, behind his gate. "No problem," he said, opening his front door and directing me outside. "You can get them from here." I sensed that this was a command that I should stroll across the front of his house, across his driveway, stark naked, and that he'd enjoy this. In response, I did so-walking slowly; trying to appear nonchalant-but I didn't put on my shorts when I found them. Instead, I picked up my clothes and strolled naked back to the porch, and engaged him in a 10-minute, irrelevant conversation-stark naked on his porch! -before dressing. I intended to communicate the message that if he enjoyed watching, I'd enjoy similar demands for exposure in the future. Message received! At the end of our conversation he growled, "Paul, from now on, leave the shorts behind."

He never again saw me, except when nude. I began to strip naked in my car as soon as I left the dormitory, and drove nude to his house. There, I'd park in his driveway (sometimes on the street) and walk naked to his front door. If he wasn't home, I'd cross the driveway to let myself in the side yard. The facade that I was privately jacking off was abandoned. Even if I knew he was home, I'd jerk off on the patio on every visit. He'd greet me on the patio later, ignoring the obvious cum drying on my chest.

I called one Saturday, and Bob told me that I was welcome, but "others" might be there. "It shouldn't interfere with anything you do, they'd understand," was the command. I began my nude exposure in the sun, before becoming aware of the voices of several other men. It became apparent that there were four men present, and that they were playing poker (at a table in full view of the patio, through sliding glass doors.) They stayed forever - I had to get back to campus for another obligation. My car keys were in the house so returning home would require naked passage in front of these strangers. The thought made me turgid.

Totally nude, semi-hard, I strolled into the house. My host sabotaged any quick escape: "We were just breaking up. Paul, meet the guys."

The next Saturday was even better; they invited me in to fill the place of a man who had to leave. Naked among fully clothed men, I played poker for an hour or more.

Once, I arrived to find a note on the front door which said, "Had to leave ... but come on over to [address] ... usual attire ... others there ... see you soon."

Again, I had received a command to escalate my perform-ance: a naked arrival at a stranger's house. I wasn't at all sure that I could do this. When I found the address, there were cars parked all over the street, apparently a party was in progress. I had to park several houses away. Sitting in my car naked, I con-sidered leaving, but my cock was becoming turgid. My gonads demanded that I proceed.

Hoping I had the right house, I stepped out into the street, and strolled slowly up to the front door. I rang the doorbell nude. Posed with my hands behind my back. Felt my heart beat rapid-ly ... and my cock stiffen. There was a long wait before the door opened. A stranger opened the door, but welcomed me in. I soon realized I was at a party - a BBQ - with 20 or so other men. Everyone else was dressed, but none was nonplused by my nudity (had they been forewarned?) I guessed that I was part of the entertainment.

I understood my role, and circulated among the others as if my nudity were as normal as their clothing. I met one of my current professors, but he seemed fine with my exposure. Got lots of sun (although my tan by then was already complete.) I stayed until the last guest had left.

Driving home naked, of course-I realized that the summer had begun my education as an exhibitionist. More advanced courses were to come. And I wanted an advanced degree.

Paul M., California

Image from Naked Magazine Issue 3.4

A Friend in Need

================

Not far from my home is one of the prettiest stretches of rural America. It is known as the Oley Valley, and is famous for its 200-year-old farmhouses, old brick churches and its quaint covered bridges. A friend of mine named Terrence rents a house there. He knows about my interest in nudity and exhibitionism, and one day he called me with a proposition.

Winston, a friend of his in the Oley Valley whom I had never met, had been in the dumps all that summer. He had broken up with a lover of many years, and Terrence thought his friend needed a dose of excitement to chase away his blues. Terrence proposed I visit Winston and take off my clothes - put on a little show for him! Terrence gave me a phone number and told me to call Winston if I was interested.

Boy, was I ever! I have a nice body and a big cock, and I've always loved to have people look at me naked. To me, there is no bigger thrill in the world than standing in front of someone with my clothes off, feeling his eyes run over my body. I called Winston and eagerly set a time to meet him a couple nights later. I told him that if he didn't mind, I'd like to arrive stark naked. He told me he'd like me to stay that way my entire visit so he wouldn't even have an image in his mind of what I looked like dressed, even after I'd left.

The night I drove to the Oley Valley it was warm but a light rain was falling. Once I was well beyond the city, I eased to the side of the road and stepped out of the car for a minute. I pulled off my T-shirt, yanked off my shorts and kicked off my shoes. I tossed the bundle of clothes inside the car and resumed the drive, feeling the damp night air swirl against my skin.

Winston had given me directions to his property and told me where to park behind his barn. As I drove into his driveway, I saw a figure heading across the yard. A pool of light from floodlights on the side of the barn showed me where I was supposed to park. They illuminated the car as if it were onstage. I brought the car to a stop and let the car door swing open. I could not see anything beyond the glare of the lights. I knew Winston was standing in the wide opening of the barn door, but he had disappeared into the surrounding darkness.

The light exposed every inch of my body as I stepped from the car, and I could almost feel the heat of his eyes on my skin. But I wanted Winston to see more than an unclad body coming toward him. I wanted him to see me erect and sexual, and my cock was responding fast. I slammed the car door. I stood there for a moment, the raindrops glistening against my skin while my cock began to swell. I walked slowly toward the barn. Each step made my cock more rigid. When I came to within 10 feet of the encircling darkness I stopped. I could see him now just inside the barn door. I spread my legs, thrust my hips toward him and wiggled my stiff cock in the wet air, silently begging him to look at it.

"I sure hope you're Winston," I said.

"Here," he responded, "I brought you a towel."

I joined him in the protection of the barn and dried off. That's when I noticed a sports car parked inside. It gave me an idea. I discovered that if I stood on its rear bumper and jumped a couple of inches, I could grasp an overhead beam. I hung there for a few moments, spread my legs and swung back and forth.

"Whatever you do," I said, "please don't stop looking at my cock."

"Let's go into the house," said Winston.

"I'll get you a beer."

Winston's house has been splendidly restored and modernized. In the living room, recessed lighting in the ceiling illuminate the area in front of the fireplace. I stood bathed in that light as Winston handed me an opened beer bottle and settled onto the sofa. His eyes tore into my cock as it stood hard against my abdomen.

I let the beer bottle come to rest against my erect cock. The shaft of the wet bottle and the shaft of my pulsing dick were practically the same size. When I brought them together, I imagined I heard a sizzle. Winston sprawled on the sofa and let out a quiet moan.

I stood beneath the overhead spotlight and began to masturbate. I loved what I was doing and let waves of sexual feeling roll over me. My heart pounded and my breath came in rasps. Never in my life had I felt so exposed.

More than a few minutes passed. I remember I put on quite a show. I let Winston look up my butt and examine the region behind my balls.

Finally, without taking his eyes off my cock, Winston drained the last of his beer and said, "How'd you like to go for a ride?"

Winston grabbed my cock for the first time and used it to lead me through the house to the back door. He pulled me across the yard and up to the barn. As I got into the front seat of his car he announced, "I'll give you a tour of the Oley Valley." Winston switched on the dashboard light, and I was surprised to find it was inverted to illuminate the crotch. I sat holding my cock perpendicular to the seat as we roared off into the night. Somehow, Winston managed to keep the car on the road!

A few minutes later we came to one of Oley's covered bridges. Winston drove to the middle of it and applied the brakes.

"Would you like to get out?" he asked. Did I ever! I would have walked across the continent without clothes just then. I didn't want to ever pass another moment without someone looking at my cock. I bounded from the car and ran in the headlights to the end of the bridge.

Beyond the roof, it was still raining. I danced in the raindrops for a minute and refreshed myself before returning to the shelter of the bridge. But the shower did nothing to tame my hard-on.

Winston had remained watching me from behind the steering wheel. I walked back to the car and knelt on the hood. I could see he was jacking off in the front seat.

"C'mon," he said softly through the open window. "Get in. We have people to visit."

A few minutes of travel brought us to Terrence's house. I'd been there a couple of times before but never without clothes. The thought of walking in there naked, flashing the biggest erection of my life, filled me with more lust than I could have imagined.

Terrence was more than expecting us. Two friends of his

whom I had never met were waiting for us, too. They sat on the couch with their arms draped around each other's shoulders. They were wide-eyed when I walked through the front door without clothes.

Terrence uncapped a couple of beers and passed them around. I found a bar stool to perch myself upon and opened my legs wide. I didn't touch myself. I just let my cock fill the room. Every few seconds I moved a fraction of an inch to give a new view.

It was so hot. Nobody spoke. Nobody took their eyes off my nude body as it squirmed in front of them atop the stool. Terrence took his cock out of his pants and began to jack off. After a while, Winston did the same thing. But it was Terrence's two friends who had grown really excited. "Gotta strip," one of them finally said as he rose from the sofa and shed his clothes.

The other stripped, too, and they fell on each other in a writhing heap on the sofa. And the whole time, they never took their eyes off me.

Just when I thought I'd blow a load if I touched my cock, Winston announced that it was time to leave. We drove back to his house, and he led me upstairs to his bedroom. He told me to stretch out on the four-poster bed in the middle of the room and he switched on a floodlight he'd tied to one of the posts. He picked up a video camera, aimed it in my direction, and said, "Now cum." I don't think he got more than three pictures before I spurted all over my torso.

I saw Winston twice after that. One time, I visited his office in the evening after everyone else had gone home. I walked off the elevator naked in Winston's building and found my way to the suite where he works and masturbated for him lying across his desk. Another time, I met him naked in broad daylight at a lonely overlook near his home and spent several hours climbing rocks and exploring the woods with him.

Soon after that, Winston repaired his relationship with his former lover, but we still talk on the telephone now and then. We consider each other friends. The neat thing about our friendship is that it has been entirely clothes-less on my part. Winston has no image in his mind of what I look like dressed. That makes me hard just thinking about it.

Robert, Allentown, PA

Encounter at Paradise

================

In 1994, I was a 56-year-old gay Florida nudist who occasionally went to the Paradise Lakes Nudist Resort for relaxation and naturally, voyeurism. One day in the early spring, although the weather was marginal, I decided to make the 30-mile trip as my lover was working, and I was bored. These trips were always refreshing but had never produced any erotic liaisons.

I had not been at the resort long before it began to rain. Moving inside a screened area, I pondered whether I should stay. However, the rain which never came down hard, abated, and as I had paid $8.46 to get in, I returned outside. I had hardly gotten my crossword puzzle out and my towel stretched over the lounger before a fellow with the penis of my dreams pulled his lounger over next to mine and introduced himself as Tom. While introducing myself to him (my name is Tom also), I observed that this 30-something-year-old who had this fantastic penis was already semi-erect. His body was hairy and muscular, and his face was handsome. Could he possibly be gay?

As we talked, he began to massage lotion onto his chest, his shoulders, and eventually his groin. When he reached his penis, he oiled it profusely, lifting the thick shaft in order to rub lotion onto his testicles, which had been shaved. His dick had become even larger by then. As we continued to talk, I had trouble listening to his conversation because of the distraction of his naked body which I longed to touch. Would I dare?

"Have you ever been to the sauna?" he asked.
"I didn't know there was one," I replied honestly.

"If the weather clouds up again, maybe we should go over there," he suggested.

I agreed and that's exactly what we did a few minutes later.

When we arrived at the sauna, it was full of mostly older, paunchy men. One woman opened the door while we were in there, but she retreated when she saw the overwhelming odds. Unaccustomed as I was to basking in a sauna, it became unbearably hot after about twenty minutes, and, when I suggested we leave, Tom agreed but asked if I would then like to canoe out onto the lake. I remembered a friend, who had visited Paradise, telling me that sex could be had on the opposite side of the lake, and I was hoping perhaps that's what was going to happen.

In order to use the canoeing equipment, we were required to wear life vests. When I looked at Tom in his red-orange vest, I noticed that covering his chest only accented the pendulous object below. We were rowing in the middle of the lake when Tom asked when I had known my marriage was not going to work, to which I replied, "On my wedding night, but it took me twenty more years to admit that I was gay."

It was the reply he was looking for as he said, "That's what I wanted to know. I pulled my lounger next to yours because I think you have a gorgeous penis, and I'm dying to hold it." As the feeling was mutual, we immediately shifted ourselves in the canoe and reached for each other's dick. His "monster," which had immediately become even longer and thicker, was pulsing and curving straight up his belly. I grasped it firmly, feeling the strength of this magnificent object. My penis curved downward and fit into the palm of his hand marvelously. I gasped as his hand closed around it, pulling gently, continuing to express admiration.

Reaching the far shore, we beached the canoe and shifted even closer to each other, continuing to explore each other's sexual apparati. The head of his penis was huge and felt smooth in my hand. He tended to my penis as I stroked his, admiring the girth of this admirable piece of flesh. I was mesmerized by the lift of his dick as it reached above his navel and pulsated in my hand. Eventually he began to show signs of approaching ejaculation, and he urged me to pull on his testicles. As I did, he leaned back and began moaning ecstatically. When he came, the semen exploded all over his chest and onto the life vest he was wearing. What a marvelous experience in the outdoors beside a lake! As his erection abated, he laughed about this being the first time he had ever had sex in a canoe. I was still holding his penis, rubbing some of his semen onto my chest. Then we headed back to the shore and returned to our lounges.

Before the day was over, we had once again gone to the sauna which this time we found empty. When Tom became erect, I masturbated him a second time, happy to have another chance to hold that piece of manhood. What a marvelous afternoon, and it was all safe sex.

Tom and I correspond as he lives in Phoenix, Arizona. He has visited me once since that wonderful summer afternoon, and his penis, which I learned he calls "George," was just as beautiful standing up in my bed as "he" was standing up against the backdrop of Paradise Lakes Nudist Camp.

Tom C., St. Petersburg, FL

Image from Naked Magazine Issue 3.2

Neptune's Son
================

This year has literally been awash with naked encounters that were unexpected and really exciting. From our balcony in St. Maarten, French West Indies, looking at the azure surf with its color disturbed only by the inky blotches of seaweed that lay eerie shadows across the bottom of the bay. I write about my most recent encounter.

The waves are crashing against the coral shelf right below our window. The pounding, pounding, pounding of the frothy surf defines the life of this place. I write about this encounter completely naked on our balcony with my partner at my side. We have just retuned from a seven-day sail around the islands of St. Maarten and St. Barth. Four of us took a bare boat, which means we sailed the 45-foot sloop ourselves without a captain or crew. It also meant we could be naked as much as we wanted to be. Naked in the French West Indies is easy and anyone wanting to be totally free of clothing should come here. No embarrassment, no harassment just acceptance.

It would be hard to be here and not have your encounter involve the sea. Mine did. I had taken a motorized fishing boat to a cluster of rocks that mark the entrance of the bay at Grand Case, FWI. The rocks, which reached forty feet into the sky, was buffeted from the north by the waves of the channel separating St. Maarten and Angilla. But the south side where we were was calmer. We had gone there to snorkel. There were several other boats tied to buoys in the area.

I stripped off the tiny bit of a swimming suit I had on and

dove off the side of the boat. I had both goggles and snorkel firmly clutched in my right hand. I took time to adjust the mask so fog would not cloud what I hoped was going to be a spectacular view of fish, coral and an underwater world. I left behind my flippers and instead wore Tennis shoes so I could walk onto a small rocky beach attached to the reef at the right of the rocks.

When you put your mask on, a spectacular underwater world is revealed. What was closed becomes open. It seems trite to say but a whole new mysterious kingdom allows the snorkeler to come inside. The only caution to mention is your butt can become very burned. Make sure that waterproof sunblock (high UV rated) is slathered thickly on all parts of your body. Especially those that rarely see the sun. The Caribbean sun is intense.

I swam and looked down into the l0-footdeep water to see purple fish, yellow fish and others. These slippery creatures scurried in and out of the rocks. I looked ahead to see another diver. He like me was naked but unlike me he was totally bronze from the top of his wavy black Mediterranean hair to his toes. I came up to clear my goggles because this was a creature I had hoped to see. Quickly I had my face back in the water and was following my creature toward the rocks.

As opposed to swimming off, he seemed to wait for me. He slowly swam toward the tiny beach. I swam closely behind him. I was memorized by the swaying of his bronze cock and his full, plump sack. Even the hair on his sack was fun to watch as it reached out. His asshole, tight and dark, appeared every now and then as he did a slow, methodical frog kick. I could feel my own cock stiffening. He swam and I followed. He would stop and let me get close but never close enough to touch. Once when I was close he let his Michelangelo's "David" - like hand stroke his uncut cock, as if adjusting it. I smiled at this enticement. He suddenly dove down to the bottom to snag a prize. I watched as he descended and ascended. He came up close to me and put the red and white coral into my hand. He swam away with muscles flexing as he reached to touch the smooth rocks in front of the tiny beach. He carefully stepped onto the pebbles.

I, too, reached the rocks and stepped up, but not nearly as gracefully as did he. I sat on a rock that kept my lower half below the waterline. He tread carefully to a spot on the sand and sat down. His bronzed body was elegant and glistening from the salty water. He stroked that bronze cock a couple of times. He looked from side to side with our eyes locking only momentarily. His magnificent cock was totally erect. He played and stroked and finally got down to pleasure. I didn't move as he worked himself to explosion. With a beautiful grimace, he shot pure white. There was momentary calm before he stepped past me and dove into the sea. He swam strongly toward his boat. He never spoke.

When I was back in the boat, my partner asked what I had been doing by the island. I realized he had not seen Neptune's son. I laughingly told him I was looking at gorgeous sea creatures. He laughed as he turned the dingy back toward our anchored sailboat.

I know what I described was not a dream because that same night we were in Marigot, FWI for dinner and I saw him again. Our eyes locked again but he didn't seem to recognize me. I now have a new appreciation for the creatures of the sea.

Seth w., Oakbrook, IL

Hiking Hard-ons

============================

During a visit to upstate New York last summer, I spent a couple of days along a small-secluded country stream working on my all-over tan and enjoying the natural scenery (which included numerous good looking hunks in their natural state!).

The main skinny-dipping area had a sandy beach that attracts couples and families, but I headed downstream where most of the single males gather among the rocks. I picked out a spot near an unoccupied blanket and set up for the day. I decided to take a hike down the long trail that runs further through the woods and down along the river.

About halfway down the trail, I spotted a guy coming toward me. He wore only a pair of hi-top sneakers and carried a small radio-cassette attached to a pair of earphones. He appeared to be in his mid-20's with blond hair and a well-toned physique. He also had a raging hard-on that swung gently from side to side as he walked. My own equipment began to stir as we passed each other, but we both continued going our own way.

When I returned to my blanket, I discovered that the guy on the trail was the owner of the blanket I had set up near. After a while, we struck up a conversation. Eventually we got around to the subject of "hiking hardons."

I told him that I do a lot of naked hiking, but any arousal is usually short lived, even with manual stimulation, as the body puts much of its energy into other functions during a brisk hike.

He then told me what his secret was.

He has several cassette tapes of hot encounters, including 900 telephone recordings and vocals from porn videos. During his hikes, he listens to these tapes to get extra stimulation to keep himself up. He sometimes plays a tape at bareass beaches, where public manual stimulation would be frowned upon. This makes it appear that he is having an involuntary erection. After a few moments, he will lay over on his stomach to feign hiding himself once he has given his neighbors a good look. He even gave me a demonstration, which led to a mutual release.

So all you hot exhibitionists out there, run out and get yourself a portable cassette player, earphones and some hot cassette tapes and have yourself lots of "hiking hardons" this summer!

Bill, Kittery, ME NM

Family Weekend

================

I thought you would be interested in this family encounter I had last year.

Last summer, my father announced that he wanted to spend his 65th birthday by going on an all-male weekend to the family cabin in the Adirondack Mountains of upstate New York. So my brothers and I made arrangements at our jobs to be free that week. On Friday afternoon we all piled into the minivan and headed north. There were seven of us: my dad, my brothers Craig (41) and Mike (36), me (34), and my nephews, Gerard (19), Tony (15), and Jimmy (9).

I had not been to the cabin in about ten years. I usually spend my summer weekends on Fire Island enjoying the naked tanned bodies on the beach and experiencing debauchery in the famed Meat Rack.

The ride up was long but it was a little like old times, at least for my brothers and Dad. We played Sinatra and Bennett on the cassette player and had fun seeing who could spot the license plates of the different states along the thruway.

We arrived late that evening, lit a fire, made some microwave pizza and drank beer, wine, and soda. We turned in early because we all knew that the wake up call from Dad would come at 6 a.m. so that we could be the first fishermen on the lake.

After fishing for a couple of hours my brother Mike and I

decided to return to the shore and sun and swim. We laid our blankets on the ground and removed our clothes. Our cabin is on a very secluded spot on the north shore of a large lake. When we were young we always skinny-dipped there with our cousins. After around an hour my brother Craig returned with his sons Gerard and Tony. Dad had stayed out for a while longer with Jimmy.

Craig took off his shorts and jumped into the lake. Gerard seemed a little hesitant at first, I guess because he had never been naked in front of his uncles before, but he soon followed his father's lead. Tony left his trunks on and sat on the bank by Mike and I. Soon after, Dad and Jimmy returned and Dad joined us. Jimmy and Tony went up to the cabin, but came back shortly, both naked too. It was obvious that Tony was a little self con-scious. He was in the middle of puberty and his cock had just started to be surrounded by a nice black bush.

I sat back and observed the situation. I found it so fasci-nating to look at the naked bodies of three generations of males in my family. We had been taught by our father that exercise and eating well was important early in our lives, so my brothers and I all have pretty good physiques. My nephews all looked good, too. It was fun silently comparing cock and ball sizes (Dad and Gerard had the biggest ones), and the pubic hair patterns of all of us.

We walked back to the house for lunch without putting on any clothes. The rest of the weekend was spent pretty much nude and we all had a great time. The only embarrassing moment came while we were watching a movie on the VCR and observed a hot scene between Susan Sarandon and Kevin Costner in a bathtub. Tony got an impressive instant erection and fled from the room. (Thank God I am not 15 anymore!)

I hope that we all can go back this August to celebrate again. But I am afraid that Mom, my sisters in-law and nieces will insist on joining us. If that happens, I guess I'll go to Fire Island instead! Fishing isn't really my thing.

John, Brooklyn, New York

Image from Naked Magazine Issue 2.4

First Nude Experience

===============

Thanks for the inspiration! Because of NAKED MAGA-ZINE and the readers' adventures, I finally got up the nerve to live out one of my dreams!

Living in a smaller town in Kansas, I have little contact with other gay men and no good place to get naked. I have also always felt that I was skinny and not much to look at, but I decided this year for my summer vacation that I would go to Timberfell Lodge in Tennessee. I had seen it profiled in your magazine and wrote to them asking about their activities. I decided to take the plunge!

I arrived there on Friday, the first day of their annual Nude Weekend, so that I couldn't "chicken out" of my very first socially nude adventure. After I checked in, toured the grounds and set up my campsite, I was ready! I stripped off my shorts, threw a towel over my shoulder and headed for the pool. I was very excited and nervous about this totally new experience and I entered the pool area very timidly. The first group of guys I met were very friendly and, after brief introductions, I joined their conversation. I soon discovered that visiting with a group of gay men was not much different than visiting with anyone else, except for the obvious honesty and sincerity of these men.

I spent the rest of the weekend lounging, swimming and hiking naked and soon grew accustomed to the feeling. I also began to realize that no matter what I thought of my body, others found me attractive and I had to politely refuse some of the unwelcome advances.

After the weekend, there was only a small group of guests remaining and I developed a daily naked routine for the rest of the week. After a quiet breakfast at my camp, I would ride my bicycle several times up and back the quarter-mile-long road to the main lodge. I enjoyed the exercise and other guests (and staff members) who were on the porch of the lodge seemed to enjoy the view!

After I put my bike away, I would smear on the sunblock, take a book to the lounge chairs around the pool, read and soak up the sun for an hour or two. By then, other guests and off duty staff members would have arrived at the pool and I would be ready to swim or play a game of water volleyball. We spent the afternoons visiting and swimming or floating on air mattresses around the pool, some of the guys chasing the sun while others retreated to shade.

At the beginning of the week, I had been very self-conscious about all the sexual comments that were directed toward me, but by the end of the week I was feeling much more comfortable and confident. In fact, I began to look forward to any comments and tried to position myself so the guys who were most interested could see what they liked. I was thrilled when I realized I could get other guys excited just by floating around the pool on an air mattress tanning my buns.

In the evening, the other guests would go to the lodge for a gourmet dinner and I would fix something at my camp. Then I would take a walk and watch the birds, rabbits or deer, and enjoy the peace and quiet of the resort.

After dinner, we would all gather at the pool again for a party, and some of the staff members and I would try to get a volleyball game started in the warm waters of the pool. We often played until one or two in the morning!

All-in-all, it was a fabulous week for me. I have never felt so comfortable in a group of new friends. I have also never been naked for a whole week or been the object of so much attention, but I have never enjoyed myself so freely and completely either. I can't wait for the next time!

Thorn M., Hutchinson, KS

Image from Naked Magazine Issue 2.4

Hot Friday Night

===============

First, just let me say that I have been a nudist for several years. I enjoy the freedom and comfort of being naked, and I usually spend all my time at home in the buff. In the last several months, I have extended my nude lifestyle to the great outdoors and occasionally I take long drives totally in the nude. This is about one of my recent naked experiences.

It all started one very warm Friday evening last summer. It wasn't warm, it was hot! I had nothing planned for the evening, so I thought about maybe watching a movie or two. So I pulled on a T-shirt, sandals, and a pair of cutoffs for a quick trip to the video store.

While I was out renting a couple of movies, a severe thunderstorm came up, and by the time I returned home, the electricity was off. "No movies tonight," I thought.

I soon realized that I had gone off to the video store with only my car key and no house key, expecting to use the garage door opener to re-enter my house. Now here I was locked out of my house, it was raining buckets, the temperature was over 90 degrees, and the humidity was 100 percent. Boy, was I ever pissed!

About that time, my neighbor Keith arrived home from work. I explained my predicament, and he invited me in to wait for the electricity to come back on.

Keith is about 6'3", has curly dark hair, deep blue eyes,

and a weightlifter's body. In fact, he has his own weight room in his home. I had watched him many times mowing his grass, washing his cars, or working around the yard wearing just gym shorts or cut-offs, and I was mightily impressed with the condition of his body, especially his smooth hairless chest and washboard abs. I yearned to see more, but as we had become friends, we had never even discussed nudity, much less that I was a nudist myself.

After we had been sitting in Keith's living room for some time, he suddenly said that he couldn't stand the heat any longer, and had to get out of the dress shirt and tie that he had worn to work. He excused himself and went into his bedroom.

Of course, I assumed he was going to change into something cooler and more comfortable. Did he ever! Imagine my surprise when this Greek Adonis walked back into the living room bare-butt naked! He began to stammer out an explanation, telling me that he often was naked at home, and hoped that it didn't make me uncomfortable. I quickly interrupted and assured him that I had no problem with his nudity, and that on the contrary I was a nudist myself, and volunteered to join him.

I quickly stood up and shed what few clothes I was wearing.

We spent the remainder of the evening talking about the naked lifestyle and exchanging some of our naked stories. We were both surprised that neither of us had even suspected that the other liked to go naked.

After the electricity came back on around 2 a.m., we decided to watch one of the movies that I had rented. We did so sitting side by side on his sofa in all our naked glory. After the movie, I even walked back home naked.

We have become close friends and continue to visit each other, and always in the nude. Frequently, at his house, we lift weights in the nude, and have talked about trying to find others who might be interested in starting a nudist club.

Gary, Lexington, KY

Maintenance Man Discovery

===============

I had been home from work for no more than 10 minutes (which means that I had been naked for about nine minutes!) when there was a knock on my front door. I glanced out the window and saw the air conditioner maintenance truck in my driveway. I totally forgot that I had made an appointment for spring maintenance on my air conditioning system! I quickly looked around for a pair of shorts, as I am not usually in the habit of answering the door naked. Then I thought, "What the hell?" and just opened the door.

I had no idea how "John" (which was what the name tag on his work shirt said) would react to a naked man opening the door. The first surprise was when he didn't say anything at all, except to introduce himself and to ask where the utility closet was located. I led him there and he went right to work.

Now I was intrigued, so I said something inane like, "I hope that I didn't embarrass you by my nudity. I usually go naked at home."

John hesitated only a second before he replied, "No, not at all. I'm a nudist myself, and I like to go naked at home, too." Well, I tell you my mouth dropped open! I never thought I would find another nudist so easily in this straight-laced town.

I wasn't about to let a situation like this go to waste. We started talking about being naked while John continued to work. We told each other about some of the things that we liked to do while bare-butt naked. I told him that I planned to go to the GNI

Gathering this year, and how I wished there was a nude group close by that I could join to get naked with others. Surprise number two came when John told me he was a member of a landed nudist club and that it was only about 25 miles away in the next county. John said he would telephone me back with information on joining if I wished. Hell yes, I wished!

All this time I had been trying to think of a way to get John to take his work clothes off without coming right out and asking. I mean, he was a stranger after all. It was starting to get hot in the house because the air conditioning had to be off while John worked on it, and also because of the direction our conversation had gone. I finally suggested that since it was so hot, maybe he would be more comfortable working in the nude. John replied that he was in a hurry to get to his next appointment and that he was almost finished anyway. He added that he would not normally turn down an invitation to get naked and winked. He must have noticed my disappointment.

A couple of minutes later John finished his work, turned, and stood up. The third surprise came when he bent over the kitchen counter to fill out his paperwork, and I noticed a small pink triangle hanging on the chain around his neck. I decided to take the initiative and just had to ask another question about the club. He hesitatingly admitted that, yes, it was strictly a "nude dude" club. And to top it all off, I told him that I had noticed the chain that he was wearing, and how much I liked it. I felt like I had died and gone to heaven when he admitted that he was gay and how much he liked what he had seen that evening also, with another wink.

John then said that he had to leave, as he still had three more appointments that evening, but I am sure that if he had not been in such a hurry, I could have gotten him out of his clothes. I walked him to the door in an attempt to prolong the occasion, and I invited him to come back when he had more time. At the door, he turned toward me, gave me a little hug, assured me that he would be back, and climbed into his truck. I stood in the doorway bare-butt naked, and waved as he drove out of sight.

Kelty, Lexington, KY

Myrtle Beach Mischief

===============

I was about 26-years-old, 5'10" and 135 lbs. when I stayed at a large beach hotel in Myrtle Beach, South Carolina. I was spending a week in Myrtle Beach for summer vacation around the 4th of July. None of my friends wanted to come along because it was about 400 miles from where I lived in Virginia, so I went by myself.

The hotel was right on the Atlantic Ocean and along the main boulevard about five miles south of the center of town (toward the end of the hotel strip). My room was on the seventh floor, on the side of the hotel that faced the ocean. The room had a balcony and floor-to-ceiling windows facing the water. Everyone on the beach could see you if you stood on the balcony. The balcony had very thin railings, so if you stood naked up there, everything you had would be exposed to people on the beach below. On one side of the hotel was a large pool. This was just at the base of a stairwell leading from the ocean view rooms. A gate separated the pool area from the beach and ocean. Steps led down from the gate to the beach and to the ocean.

Early one morning (about 2 a.m.), I decided to go skinny-dipping in the pool. I stripped naked and stood on the balcony, listening. The only thing I could hear was the gentle lapping of the waves on the shore. I decided to leave the door to the room unlocked so I wouldn't have to carry a key. I checked to make sure the door wouldn't close accidentally and lock me out. Then, I listened to be sure that no one was in the hall.

Quietly, I stepped out into the hall - completely naked! It was warm that early July morning. I closed the door part-way, then I wandered past four or five rooms to the stairwell. I carefully opened the stairwell door and listed to be sure there were no voices or footsteps. Then I ran down the seven flights of stairs to the pool level. I listened again to be sure there were no voices out by the pool since I couldn't see the pool from my room! I got to the pool level and, finding no one there, jumped right into the pool. It felt exhilarating to be swimming in the warm water totally naked! There were about 150 rooms facing the pool. I quickly checked to be sure there wasn't anyone out on any of balconies. There didn't appear to be, so I continued swimming. It was fun. I swam backstroke and sidestroke for about 10 minutes. The warm water rushed all over my naked body. I loved seeing my dick slice through the water as I swam backstroke!

I looked up and saw another cute young guy sitting on one of the balconies looking down at me. I guess he had opened the door to his balcony very quietly because I didn't hear him open the door. He had shorts on but no shirt. Even though it was dark, I could tell that he was young and pretty good looking. I was pretty sure he saw me, but I didn't care. He would never have been able to make it down to me that quickly from where his room was, maybe five or six floors above the pool. I got out of the pool and ran back up to my room along the pool deck still totally naked. If he didn't see me before, I'm sure he saw me then I got to the door of my room on the seventh floor just as some people came around the corner. That was close!

The next night I decided to try skinny dipping in the ocean! I again stripped naked at 2 a.m. and stood on my balcony. Occasionally some people - mostly young couples out for a late night walk on the beach would walk by, but none of them looked up to see me. I carefully opened the door and stepped out into the hallway. I heard voices, so I stepped back into the room and closed the door. I waited five or 10 minutes and opened the door again. The coast was clear, so I stepped out and started streaking completely naked toward the stairwell door, down the seven flights of stairs, out onto the pool deck, past the pool, and then through the gate out to the beach, down the steps and into the sand.

The ocean was about 20 or 30 yards away. I glanced up to see if any of the hundred rooms facing the ocean had any lights on or people on the balconies. Seeing none, I started streaking toward the ocean. I looked up and down the beach to see if anyone was around, but I didn't see anyone. It was so quiet and so dark since it was almost a new moon that night.

I swam out about twenty yards until I was well away from the shore and just listened to the waves. It was beautiful. The ocean was very warm there, about 85 degrees, even that late at night, so I was in no hurry to get out. It felt good to be swimming naked.

Then I started to worry that someone might come along and block my path back to the hotel, so I quickly swam back to shore, got out and began running for the gate. My cut 7-inch dick was as hard as a rock!

I got to the steps leading up from the beach and opened the gate. The coast was clear there was no one in the pool area. I started toward the stairwell across the pool deck. Just as I got to the door, it opened and out came a guy and his girlfriend! My heart was beating really fast. I quickly put my hand over my dick and said, "Hello!" to them, and kept going. I know they both looked around and saw my bare bubble butt as I ran up the seven flights of stairs and listened at the top for voices in the hallway. Hearing none, I opened the door and streaked down the hallway back to my room.

My heart was beating so fast and I was breathing so hard, but it was an incredible rush! I stepped out on the balcony to see if I could see the couple that had surprised me but they had continued on down the beach. I really enjoyed skinny-dipping at that hotel and got naked and went skinny-dipping in the pool on several occasions thereafter. It was fun to be more daring and stay out longer each time!

I still remember this as one of my favorite summer vacations.

Tyler, Orange County, CA

Naked Driver Hunt!

===============

I have been a nudist as long as I can remember. My dad used to swim and "parade" around the house naked, much to my mother's annoyance. I guess I got my desire to be naked from him, and I'm grateful for that. I only dress out of necessity-work, shopping, weather. I enjoy driving naked on long trips, and would like to relate one especially interesting adventure.

The highway between Phoenix, where I live, and Los Angeles can be pretty dull; with miles and miles of miles and miles. I always travel that road naked, and a couple of summers ago had reason to make the trip frequently to help one of my best friends move back to Phoenix from L.A. My friend is also a nudist, and enjoys being naked at home, at parties, camping, the beach, etc., but he thought driving naked was a bit "too much." He also thought I was a little strange in wanting to drive naked, and he didn't think anyone else ever did such a "silly" thing. He learned differently during this trip.

We had cause to make a quick trip together from Phoenix to L.A. Jack, my best friend, drove, and I was the passenger. I told him it would be fun to drive naked, but he said he'd rather not - but if I wanted to ride naked it was okay with him. I said that maybe I shouldn't because he wouldn't be naked with me. But he encouraged me to get naked, so of course I did!

It was a wonderful summer day, with temperatures in the 90s. The windows were down, my clothes were off and we were screaming down the highway at 85 miles per hour heading for California.

I really wanted Jack to get naked, too, and enjoy the freedom and fun of driving without a stitch, and I knew the only way I'd convince him was to spot other naked drivers and prove to him that I was not the only one who enjoyed driving in the buff.

We didn't have long to wait. The first apparently naked driver was a trucker we passed without his shirt on. He could see that I was naked in the car, and sounded his horn and waved. I got Jack to slow down and the truck driver pulled along side of us, smiling broadly and pointed to his crotch, indicating he was naked, too. Here was someone else who enjoyed driving naked, and we spotted him only 40 miles out of town. He was probably about 35 years old, dark wavy hair, hairy chest and very tan, with a great face and smile.

But one naked driver wasn't enough to convince Jack to get naked.

The next naked driver was someone whom Jack spotted. After the truck driver, I must have piqued his interest and now he was looking for them, too! We pulled up beside a large motorhome, one of the models with the door just behind the passenger seat. The window on the entry door was open and you could see the driver from the knees up, and guess what? He was naked! Beautiful white butt, tan arms and chest, maybe 40-45 years old; racing down the freeway naked in his motorhome! I don't know if he realized anyone could see him or not, but we were glad that we could.

I said to Jack, "There. Are you ready to get naked now?"

All he said was, "Maybe later."

We passed the next hour without spotting any other naked drivers. We enjoyed the time visiting, sharing our feelings and enjoying each other's company.

Just before we hit Barstow, we spotted two extremely handsome shirtless guys in a pickup truck. I was convinced they were naked too, and talked Jack into at least taking off his shirt so they'd think we were both in the buff. He agreed easily - he thought the two guys were cute and he had seen that others drive naked, too. He took off his shirt; now he was only wearing shorts (and his shorts weren't much). We caught up with the guys in the pickup - they were in their 30s and looked like construction workers. One was Hispanic, dark, 'stash, sunglasses; the other was brown haired with what looked like a dark patch of hair in the middle of his chest. They were laughing, sitting close together, and looked like they had been up to something, maybe even groping each other. When they spotted us they could see that I was naked, and I'm sure it looked like Jack was naked too. The truck sat up higher than the car, so they had a better view. They waved, smiled, and rode alongside us for 30 minutes or so, until traffic got in the way. We played a kind of highway "tag" for a few miles until they turned off, with lots of smiles and waves, a naked kinship at 85 miles per hour!

By now, Jack was convinced that I was not the only "nut" who enjoyed traveling naked, but he still wouldn't take the plunge!

About an hour later, it started to get dark. As soon as it was dark enough for headlights, Jack surprised me and stripped. He admitted that the reason he hadn't gotten naked before was because he'd had a raging-hard-on since I had taken my clothes off at the start of the trip. And sure enough, by the light of the dashboard I could see his beautiful white dick standing straight up between his legs. I don't know if it was me, driving naked, the other naked drivers, the closeness we were sharing, our friendship, or just that he was horny, but I was glad he was finally naked beside me.

We drove the rest of the way to L.A. naked, touching each others' thighs, chest, shoulders, arms with warm gentle hands. It was a moment of deep sharing for two loving friends. We've become much closer friends having shared this experience. We've even repeated it several times since then.

Ray S.., Phoenix, AZ

Nudepourri!

=================

Instead of a long, single story, I have a series of shorter true experiences to share. I have a motive for telling them, which I will divulge at the end.

** While waiting for the trams to take visitors back to the parking area at Busch Gardens in Virginia one hot afternoon, a nicely built teenager beside me jumped up to sit on the low fence which corralled us into lines. Facing me and no one else, he wore brief shorts, shoes and little else. Immediately, I noticed the tip of his penis peeking out one leg of his shorts. As he opened and closed his crotch, as guys do for enjoyment, two inches of his expanding organ eventually protruded from his shorts, for only me to enjoy. I was wearing dark glasses so I could "safely" watch from the corner of my eye, but I never acknowledged him and that beautiful sight.

** While on a rafting trip on the Colorado River, I had struck up a casual friendship with Gary, a nice guy who was alone on the trip. One evening while our group camped along the river, I decided to stroll alone in the trees along the bank, possibly hoping to jerk off if I found the privacy. Eventually I ran into Gary in a clearing, wearing nothing. He turned his smile, his smooth body and his semi-erect penis toward me, almost inviting me to stop and "talk." I nervously apologized for bothering him and went on my way. His smiles the next day were even warmer, but I stubbornly showed no obvious interest.

** One warm day in San Diego, I parked in the far end of the mall parking lot where we employees are requested to park.

As I walked around a few cars, I encountered a nice guy I knew vaguely from work, standing stark naked in the warm sun by his van, cradling his 8-incher in his palm while taking a majestic leak. Maybe he had been changing clothes for work. He looked up at me with a faint smile and, amazingly, showed no surprise. My face flushed and my heart raced as I took a quick look, but I hurried on my way as if I hadn't noticed him, while he finished peeing.

**   Also in San Diego, I once went to a car wash where guys in tiny shorts finished off the wash job, inside the car and out, with a towel. The guy who was to finish off my car drove it a short distance so that the driver's door was in the sun and facing a vacant lot. I stood by the open door while he sat sideways in the driver's seat and started toweling with his nice fuzzy legs sticking out toward me.

Leaning back to reach, his knees soon came far apart as he toweled my windows and dash. One very fine penis and pair of balls were soon on display in the leg of his brief shorts. I guess I felt as safe observing the wonderful spectacle as he did providing it for me. As he slid over to the other seat, his shorts were pulled down around his knees. His partial erection, protruding from a perfectly beautiful crotch, was now totally uncovered and writhing in the warm afternoon sun. I tipped him generously, and he said, "Come back some day!" I never did.

**   Once in my college days, I had a hospital job which required some of us to bunk overnight on call. Double-decker bunks were provided for us guys. I was still half asleep in a lower bunk early one morning, when a perfect specimen about three years older than me walked up stark naked, leaned his chest against the top bunk and talked for a long time with the guy bunking above me. His beautiful cock and balls were nested in a mound of pubic hair glistening in the morning sun right in front of me. I sat up and stared at the gorgeous sight for 15 minutes while he kept his penis slightly erect with an occasional massage with his hand. I had never looked at another man's naked crotch so long at such a close range. What ecstasy!

When he finally walked away, he looked back at me, pretended to notice me for the first time, and then smiled coyly. The look on his face said, "Well, what did you think?" I pretended not to have noticed him and his magnificent crotch.

** I had just finished visiting the Vigeland Park in Oslo, Norway, where dozens of very naked and anatomically correct males (and females) are on display in statue form. There was almost no crowd, and I sat on a bench near the gate awaiting the bus. I heard the voices of several happy young men behind me, and turned to look. There were three lovely young Norwegian men, obviously drunk, urinating together into a storm sewer. They had completely unbuttoned their pants and lowered their underwear slightly to pee. When they saw me admiring them, all three lifted their shirts, lowered their pants to midthigh and started peeing higher in the air. Just as I was getting nerve to take out my camera, they laughed out loud and turned their dangling penises toward me for a few seconds. They then dressed and quickly disappeared.

Prior to reading NAKED MAGAZINE, I assumed I was alone in my "perverted misery." I love to be naked, but am very shy about it. I like to pull out my penis briefly where I shouldn't, walk naked in the dark, and run stark naked in nature. I have never been caught doing it. I love to admire the naked bodies of other men, but only when it is a two-way affair, with both men seeming to enjoy it. I would never enjoy peeking through a hole in the wall of a shower or restroom, but I respect those who do.

NAKED MAGAZINE has allowed me to realize that there are other normal men like myself who enjoy the same things I do. I know now that there are some naked men out there to whom I can safely say, "You really have a nice body!" or "You should be proud of that magnificent crotch!" without making them think I am a pervert or just out for sex. In the true stories I have told, I now regret that I felt so inhibited in my desire to admire naked men directly, comment positively about a nice penis, or even touch the beautiful naked men I have met accidentally. Since I began reading NAKED MAGAZINE, I have met no new naked men yet, but at least I feel good about myself, and will have the confidence to show my appreciation of naked men in some way in the future.

Thanks a lot, NAKED MAGAZINE!

Mark W., Dayton, Ohio

Office Lap Dance

===============

I have a story about being naked at work.

Once I was working for a company that was on the verge of bankruptcy, it was Christmas time, morale was quite low, and they could not afford Christmas bonuses. They instead offered the employees two extra days off, at either Christmas or New Years.

Well I figured everyone would want to take theirs at Christmas, and since I was not going anywhere for the holidays, I chose to take mine around New Years. As I suspected, it was dead around the office at Christmas, everyone had taken the day off.

I was at my cubicle talking on the phone to a friend, when I heard the voice of a co-worker around the corner. All of a sudden, I got really giddy (we were the only two in the area at the time) and told my friend I would call her back and quickly hung up the phone.

I spontaneously stripped off all my clothes and walked around the corner, up behind my co-worker while he was on the phone! I tapped him on the shoulder, he turned around his jaw dropped-he was stunned!

He said, "Michael put some clothes on!" while covering the telephone mouthpiece. He went back to his conversation while I paraded naked back and forth in front of him, watching me as he continued his conversation.

Eventually, I walked back to my desk and put my clothes back on. I came back after lunch, he was finally off the phone. I asked if he enjoyed what I did, and he told me he had, but that it was too bad he was on the phone and not able to enjoy it more. He then commented that I had a big dick for a short guy, to which I asked if he would like to see it again? He said, "Sure, if you would like to show me."

I went and stood across from his cubicle in the door of his boss' office (the boss was not there) and proceeded to strip down to nothing! I asked, "Do you like what you see?" "Yes!" he said. I then asked, "Do you want to see my dick hard?" He said, "If you would like to show me."

I then grabbed my already excited cock and started stroking it until it was completely hard!

"Would you like to see me cum?" He got up and said, "Sure, but do it in here." We went inside the boss' office, he locked the door as I sat on his lap totally naked, while he was fully clothed and jacked myself off to orgasm!

I have other naked stories, but this is my favorite because it involved the most risk, and it was highly erotic to me being totally naked while the other guy was fully clothed.

Michael, West Hollywood, CA

Parking Lot Exhibitionists

================

One Friday night my friend Ben and I were out dancing until 2 a.m. When we got into the car to drive home, Ben started to undress as I was driving. When he was naked, he said, "I beat you!" I stopped the car in front of a sleazy cruise bar and got naked. We sat there in the car for a few minutes, but there was no one walking by, so we left. We drove to a leather /Levi's bar not far away. We pulled into the parking lot behind the bar but didn't go inside.

It was pretty chilly so Ben put on his leather jacket and got out of the car. He walked across to parking lot to the opposite corner, pissed behind a dumpster and walked back to the car. He stood between my car and the one next to us on the passenger side. I put on my leather jacket, got out of the car and stood between the cars on the driver's side. There we were, one on each side of the car, wearing just boots and jackets, playing with our dicks. A couple of cars drove through the lot. The drivers looked at us, but they kept going.

Then a car pulled in and drove past us to the end of the lot. He stopped briefly, then started to back out to the street. This time he saw me. He stopped and watched me jack off for a couple of minutes and then shined a flashlight on me. By this time I'd forgotten how chilly it was. I just didn't notice anymore. Being watched with a flashlight shining on me was enough to keep me warm. He said," Are you going to shoot soon?" I said, "Yes, right now." I came in the parking lot, bathed in the light from his flashlight. He started to back out to the street, then stopped and came back. He said, "Come here." I walked over to his car. He reached out, grabbed my dick and pulled me up against his car.

Then he leaned over and started sucking my dick through the window of his car! Now I was standing in the middle of the parking lot wearing just boots and a jacket, getting a blow-job. While this was going on two guys walked by, looked and went on. Then someone else came out of the bar and got into his car. He backed out of the parking space and headed his car in our direction. Now the headlights were on us. He stopped briefly then drove past us slowly. The guy in the car was still sucking my dick. Shortly after this he stopped sucking, said thanks and left. I walked back to my car and realized how chilly it was, now, I got into my car to get warm.

Ben was still standing outside the car where he had been watching us. Then another car came into the lot and the driver noticed Ben. He parked two cars away from us. Ben walked over to him and was standing beside his car by the driver's door for a couple of minutes. Two guys came out of the bar and the guy in the car told Ben to walk away. He came back and got into my car. When the other two had left the lot the guy got out of his car and walked over to the passenger's side of my car. Ben got back out, still wearing just boots and a jacket. The guy dropped to his knees and started to suck Ben's dick. It must have been closing time for the bar because several people came out. Three or four walked by, looked and continued on. A couple of cars drove by, all while the guy was still sucking Ben's dick. Then someone, who apparently worked in the bar, came out and started to get into a truck that was parked across the lot directly behind us. He stopped, turned around, and looked at Ben standing there getting a blow-job. He said, "Don't get us in trouble now," got into his truck and left. Shortly after that, Ben's cocksucker friend finished what he was doing and left. Ben got into the car and we went home.

I've been back to that parking lot twice since then and played around a little. So far that first night has been the most fun, but I'm going to keep trying to top it!

Danny E., Los Angeles, CA

Image from Naked Magazine Issue 2.4

Sanctuary at the Rocks

===============

I consider it my sanctuary; my spiritual, physical, mental and emotional retreat from the world and from all the negative forces that seek to pull me down. The rocks on the James River- in conservative Richmond, Virginia- is a place I learned about only in late July of 1996 from my roommate.

I had just returned from a Saturday morning workout at the "Y" and arrived home to be greeted by my bored and "wanting to do something" roommate. "I could go for a nice run in the park," I said. "After all, I'm already warmed up."

My roommate didn't say anything for a couple of minutes, but then his face lit up with the look of a child on Christmas morning. "Let's go to the river!" he said. "To the rocks!"

Obviously confused by what he was talking about, I stood there listening while he explained about the section of the James River where gay men go to sunbathe and relax in the nude.

In the nude. Sounds like a 90s version of the old Andrews Sisters' song, but three words that set my heart a-beating and my feet a-moving! "What are we waiting for?" I said. "Let's go!" Getting to the rocks is an adventure in itself. After descending a natural staircase and crossing a long overpass (that overlooks railroad tracks that cut through a forest); one has a choice of either making his way through the woods or along the railroad tracks and then descending down to the river. Because it was getting late in the day and because we both wanted to get to the river and see some beautiful D&A (dick and ass!), we chose to go the railroad tracks route.

After making our way down a small slope from the tracks, we soon entered the forest that stood beside us, and began the trek down a winding path and through the woods.

A stream could be heard and seen in the distance, and I found myself getting stimulated by nature's sensuous wardrobe. I also wondered when the first naked man would appear. Would I have to be him? Would I be forced to remove all my clothes and declare to all the creatures of the forest that Mr. Big Dick was here? These were the questions that now had entered my mind.

"I hope you don't mind getting your shoes wet," my roommate cautioned, temporarily breaking the spell I was under. "We've got some wading to do now." Wet shoes? I thought. Was he kidding? If it meant seeing a naked man, my roommate could turn me upside down and fill every orifice of my body with water!

So we made our way across the stream that paralleled our wooded path and separated us from our Garden of Eden. Absolute heaven, I thought, as I turned and saw nothing but rocks, forest and blue sky.

Finally we arrived at what could only be described as the "real-life Gilligan's Island." That's how I describe my future sanctuary because it looked exactly like the lagoon from the classic television series. As I stood there observing the pseudo-tropical scene, I envisioned a skinny, bare-assed Gilligan making his way down to the swimming hole for his daily bath, only to find the naked Professor waiting to give him a primitive anatomy lesson. On that first visit to the rocks, my roommate and I only came across a few bare-assed men, only one of them rising up to show us his manhood.

In the weeks that followed, I went to the rocks as much as possible. By myself, I would discreetly reveal myself physically by laying totally naked on one of the many rocks. I always hoped that a semi-clothed man (or group of men) would discover me and observe my dick and balls roasting under the hot rays of the sun. Almost always my exhibitionist dreams came true and I loved giving the fellows that came along a show! Thanks for the memory'

Oh, the joys of my sanctuary! How can I describe them? From having the warmth of the sun's rays envelope my naked body, to the cool, rippling water of the lagoon making its way through my pubic hair, to the naked workout routines I do in the woods or on the rocks. I always leave my sanctuary, my Garden of Eden, feeling refreshed, renewed and most of all ... alive!

Michael D., Richmond, VA

School Days

==================

I am a blond-haired, blue-eyed exhibitionist in my late twenties. It was during high school that I first began experimenting with public nudity. Though I was never sure why, for some reason I wanted to be naked in as many places as possible at school. I was both on the crew team and acted in school theater, and often stayed on campus until after nine in the evening.

The first time I ever bared all was in the boys' locker room, naturally enough. At the time of the year and time of day that I began experimenting, there weren't any team practices going on, but the locker room was still semi-busy with students who'd stay late to use the weight room or take karate classes or play some one-on-one in the gym. I felt more comfortable at the time without a large audience, anyway.

At first, I'd just get undressed and leisurely walk around. I'd take long showers, then take even longer drying off and walking around with just a towel around my shoulders. This way, I could confront other guys in the nude and it would seem natural. My favorite encounters at this time were when I'd run into someone who was still dressed and I'd stop to make small talk while I stood there naked in front of them. My body was never "built," but I was (and still am) trim with decent sized equipment. It was quite a turn-on to me to see guys coyly checking me out as I talked to them, or used the urinals, or combed my hair in the mirror while completely naked. Slowly, I risked masturbating in the showers. With the water running, it wasn't always easy to tell if someone was approaching, but I only got caught once. Luckily, he smiled and said he understood. He began showering but I was too frightened to continue and I quickly left the showers. Oh, if I had it all over to do again ...

After awhile, the locker room became too comfortable and safe, so I began to venture to other areas on the school grounds and take off my clothes. Perhaps I'll send you some more of my campus adventures for a future issue!

L.P., Chicago, IL

The Good Old Days at the"Y"

The sight of bare-chested men on television stimulated my adolescent eyes. I fondly remember the pilot episode of the 1970s comedy, "Chico and the Man." The old man opened the bathroom door and found Chico (the late Freddie Prinz) taking a bath. After a short exchange of dialog, Chico said "Hey, you wanna look at naked men? Go to the YMCA!"

Sometime later, I read an article in some magazine relating how the Olympic games in ancient Greece were performed in the nude. The article also said that swimming in the nude is the norm at most men's clubs. This piqued my curiosity, and I recalled the statement that "Chico" had made about naked men at the YMCA.

I never played sports, so I had no outlet for seeing males in the raw. My teenage fantasies frequently consisted of men swimming in the nude at a health club. During my college years, a traveling salesman told me that the downtown YMCA in his hometown was not coed and nude swimming was the rule.

I anxiously made the four-hour journey to this YMCA during the fall of 1983. Knowing that I was about to enter the world of communal male nudism made me excited and nervous as I ascended the steps to the front door. The desk clerk gave me two towels and a locker key, along with directions to the locker room. I began placing things in my locker, when a nearby door opened.

A handsome naked man entered the locker room, water dripping from his tall, lean body. He smiled and gave a friendly hello, reaching out to shake my hand. We introduced ourselves as he began drying off using a towel which was draped over his shoulder. I told him I was visiting from out of town and he said, "Come on, I'll show you around!"

He finished drying off and threw his towel in a bin as we exited through the same door from which he had entered. We headed down a hallway and he showed me the workout room. Located directly off the sides of the workout room were doors leading to the showers, steam room, and sauna. We went back into the corridor, up two flights of stairs and crossed a landing that led onto the jogging track. The track circled the upper portion of a gym that became visible below as we made our way to the railing. A basketball game was currently in progress and we watched for a few moments before heading back to the stairs, dodging several joggers in the process.

He took me down three flights, through part of another locker room, and through several doors before reaching the swimming pool. Naked swimmers occupied three lanes and a man was standing naked at the edge of the pool adjusting his goggles. I watched with delight as he dove into the fourth lane. Feigning ignorance, I asked if it was okay to swim in the nude. "Oh sure, everybody does," he remarked, with a tone suggesting that he could not imagine men swimming any other way. We continued our conversation heading back to the locker room. He dressed and left as I sat there exhilarated by the fact that my tour guide was stark naked as he showed me around the building!

Dominating one wall of the sauna was a large window of clear glass that overlooked the workout area. I noticed two men engrossed in conversation during their workout. One of them completed his workout and started undressing on the workout floor while continuing to talk to his friend. He sat and began taking off his shoes and socks and his shirt soon followed. After a few moments the guy shed his shorts and continued the conversation wearing only a jockstrap! The jockstrap eventually found its way off and he placed his sweaty clothes in a gym bag. He stood buck naked for a few minutes and finished his conversation heading to the showers as he bade farewell to his friend. There were several other men working out and no one acted as if this man being naked on the workout floor was anything out of the ordinary.

The pool area was brightly lit and covered from floor to ceiling in green tile. One wall contained several shower heads, plus a urinal and toilet right out in the open. A nude man emerged from the pool as I began swimming in an empty lane. He walked over to the urinal, took a piss: and began taking a shower. I swam a few more laps and sat on the edge of the pool to rest and take in the sights. Looking around the room, I witnessed beautiful naked bodies swimming gracefully with bare asses protruding from the water.

I made another trip to this YMCA several weeks later and my experience was much the same. Alas, this paradise soon ended. The old building had been in disrepair for years and the new YMCA facility was near completion and would be coed. Early in 1984 the old Y closed its doors forever, thus ending its tradition of nude swimming. The building eventually met with a wrecking ball to clear the site for a parking lot. A friend was visiting the city on business several years later and passed by the new parking lot. He smiled and recalled how I, besides countless other men, had once swam in the nude where a parking lot now stood.

Naked Sam, Cincinnati, OH

Image from Naked Magazine Issue 2.4

HALF NAKED:

===============

Nudists with non-Nudist partners

The scene is familiar: Happy couples lounging on the nude beach, soaking up the sun, naked bodies everywhere. Here and there, however, a colorful dotting of fabric interrupts the sea of skin: reluctant suntanners coaxed by their partners to join them at the nude beach, but refusing to shed their shorts for that total body experience.

Many male naturists claim to have acquired their distaste for clothing early on in life, sometimes as far back as infancy. Others discover the lifestyle later in life. Regardless of when one officially becomes a nudist, what happens when a person meets that special someone who makes their heart go wild and it turns out he does not share their love for being naked? Or perhaps he even has contempt for it, finding the lifestyle distasteful.

Frequently, nudist men with non-nudist partners face additional conflict in their relationships, often brought on by the nudity issue. While some couples happily coexist with one nudist and one non-nudist partner, the rifts that develop with other couples are sometimes enough to bring on the demise of the relationship.

NAKED MAGAZINE spoke to five "half naked" couples to get their perspectives on the nudity vs. non-nudity issues facing their relationships. Some questions we sought out to answer:

What were the common problems and conflicts? Did demographics such as age, geography and length of the relationship

have any influence? And finally, what is the best way to "come out" as a nudist to your partner, and encourage him to tryout the nudist way of life? Here is what they had to say.

Half Naked: Interview I

===============

Jim D. and Paul G. Hartford, CT

As unusual as it may sound, the president of one of the country's largest and most active gay nude clubs is currently enjoying a 17-year relationship with his non-nudist partner.

Jim D., the top officer of Bare & Gay of Connecticut (B&G), says he's enjoyed being naked since he was a little kid, when he'd strip and run around in the woods near his childhood home. At 19, his first nude beach visit cemented his nudist desires. "I loved the feeling of freedom that came with it, as well as the combination of sensuous undertones that it brought," the 41-year-old says. "Ever since then, I've always sought out places where I can be nude with others, especially outdoors."

Jim's nudist practices have continued to this day and include many regular events with B&G, despite his lover Paul's apathy about the lifestyle. While Paul accepts Jim's naked desires, and even jokes about them ("He kids me about it, timing how many seconds it takes me to get my clothes off when I walk in the door!" Jim laughs.), Paul just doesn't enjoy social nudity.

"I like the outdoor events, but the sun and I don't get along," Paul says. "I work out a lot now, but having been a fat child, I still feel a little insecure about my body."

Jim was a practicing nudist long before he met Paul. "While I think he sometimes finds it a bit odd, he supports my desire to do it," Jim says. "At first, there was some question in his mind as to how much of it was an interest in nudism and how much of it was sexual opportunism, and I think he perceived it as a threat to the relationship. We've talked a lot about it and he realized the level of my commitment to him."

Paul, 38, echoes this view. "I like events that are outside, as it seems more natural to be naked," he says, "But being naked inside seems more sexual and I'm not very comfortable with that."

Paul is among the handful of non-nudist partners that NAKED interviewed who has actually given social nudity a try before deciding it wasn't for him. The couple frequently spends their vacations at clothing optional resorts and beaches so that Jim can have his nude time. "Paul will wear a bathing suit," Jim says. "But he doesn't mind that I prefer to be nude. Being nude doesn't have the same appeal to him as it does for me."

Half Naked: Interview II

===============

Phill B. and Gary L. Ft. Lauderdale, FL

Phill B. wasn't raised a nudist, but he got his first push into the lifestyle from his mother, albeit jokingly. "As a kid, I always complained about clothes-I hated them!" he laughs. "So my ma used to tell me that I should join a nudist colony. Little does she know...? "

Phill's full embracing of the naked lifestyle came very recently, after he and his lover Gary became a couple last October. In fact, Phill, 34, says he "finally stepped out of his clothes" a few months ago, something Gary, 37, had a difficult time adjusting to.

"(Nudism) is not something I've ever been greatly interested in, though I've always known about nude beaches in several areas near where I've lived," Gary says. "I've never really been that interested in going, although now that my lover is interested, I supposed I'd go. It's obviously something I will have to deal with while we are together."

Shortly after this interview was conducted, Phill told NAKED that his lover had joined him at a nude beach for the first time. They visited Haulover Beach near Miami.

"He seemed to be handling being there-still in his swimsuit-just fine," Phill says of the trip. "After a half hour he said to me, 'You know, the things that seem intimidating in thought aren't intimidating in actuality.' I was happy with his revelation until he burst my bubble: 'I think it's really silly, everyone walking around without any clothes on.'" Gary later apologized for the remark, saying he didn't really feel that way, but was trying to deal with his own intimidation.

But the greatest revelation was yet to come. "Later on, I was laying on my belly," Phill recalls, "and I turned my head toward Cary. I saw him wiping his feet off, and I thought, 'I didn't put a hand towel in the beach bag.' When I looked at what he was wiping his feet with, I saw that it was his swimsuit!" Later that evening at home I asked him, 'It wasn't really that big of a deal today, was it?' and he said that it wasn't."

While Cary has begun to take the first steps, such as visiting nude beaches with his partner, he still has some concerns about the lifestyle.

"One worry is becoming sexually aroused," Cary admits. "I'm not interested in sharing that publicly. There is still a certain perception that nudity connotes sexuality. NAKED MAGAZINE sometimes fosters that idea through its Encounters & Adventures section." But Cary's ambivalence hasn't kept Phill from living his life as naked as possible.

"I'm always naked at home," Phill says. "Cary doesn't say anything about it. When we were first together and I was nude at home, he used to think it was a teaser for making love. Now, after nine months together, he's beginning to realize that is not always why I'm nude."

Phill says that he wants to join a nude club in his area, "But I think I'd better wait on that," he adds.

"He's getting better, but Cary still thinks it's all about sex. No matter how I try explaining that nudism isn't based on sex, but being without the constraints of clothing, the exhilarating feeling of being 'natural' with other people and the acceptance of others at literally face value, he still won't buy it."

(Editor's note: Right before press-time, Phill informed NAKED that he and his lover Cary had split up. Phill is not sure whether naturism was an issue in the break-up. "Cary told me that even though he still connotes of nudism with sex, he is seeing that that really isn't correct," Phill said. "Cary also said he doubts that he will ever have the same passion for naturism that I have, but he has come to enjoy it." Phill does see some overall hope for others through his own situation. "We can change the narrow views of nudism through the simple expression of action," he said. "As long we mean what we say, our words will prove the truth through our actions.")

Half Naked: Interview III

===============

Cliff P. and Jason S. Chicago, IL

Cliff P. is a relative newcomer to the naked lifestyle. The 35-year-old was on a business trip to Vancouver five years ago and found a listing in a travel guide that gave directions to Wreck Beach, Vancouver's clothing-optional recreation area. "I had always wanted to visit a nude beach," Cliff said, "but being from the Midwest, I never really had the opportunity." So Cliff took the plunge after work one afternoon and headed to Wrecks.

"I was really nervous, and kept my shorts on at first," he recalls. "After about 20 minutes, I slipped my shorts off, and you know what? Nobody even noticed!" Cliff says within a few minutes he became more relaxed, and he "marveled at how liberating it was to be completely unencumbered of clothing, and how natural it seemed to be naked with other naked people."

Unfortunately, Cliff's partner of five years, Jason, doesn't share the same enthusiasm for social nudity. In fact, Cliff didn't tell Jason about his nudist desires "until we were well within our relationship," he says. "I 'came out' to him, so to speak, as a nudist."

Jason, who's 31, has visited nude beaches and resorts with Cliff in the past-"And he enjoyed it!" Cliff insists-but Cliff believes Jason cannot get past the "nudity equals sex" misconception that so many non-nudists have.

"For Jason, nudity is sexual," Cliff says. (Jason declined to be interviewed, but allowed his partner to fill in "his side" of the story.) "For him, being naked around other naked men for an extended period of time is sexually frustrating. He feels a lot of uncomfortable tension."

Cliff says that, at first, Jason did not understand his desires to be naked, but has warmed up to it over the years. "I'm usually naked at home, and he finds certain things odd about it," Cliff says. "If he walks into the house while I'm taking dishes out of the dishwasher naked, he starts laughing. I guess it still seems very unconventional to him."

While Jason does not enjoy naked activities to the same extent that Cliff does, Jason understands his partner's desire to be naked. "I go to nude beaches, clothing optional resorts and the GNI gathering every year," Cliff says. "My boyfriend actually encourages it now, because he knows that the nudist lifestyle is important to me."

And importantly, Cliff says there's a high level of trust in their relationship that allows Jason to breathe easy about his partner's participation at nudist functions. "We're pretty secure in our relationship," he says. "He understands that, for me, it's not about sex. I'm not looking for a new husband, or an affair. I just like to be naked."

Half Naked: Interview IV

===============

Kelly J. and Ken W. Houston, TX

Houston couple Kelly and Ken, have been together for two years. In that time, Ken has learned much about his partner's desire to remain naked, but aside from periodically going to nude beaches and resorts with Kelly, Ken doesn't subscribe to the same nudist philosophies.

"He just doesn't think it's that big of a deal," Kelly says. "Also, I'm sure he thinks most nude guys are 'trolls' only looking for sex."

Kelly discovered nudism by "doing what seemed 'natural'" "I love the feel of the sun and wind on my skin," he says. "I used to live on a farm and I would go out in the fields night and day and just strip down naked and wander around."

Thirty-one year old Kelly says he sometimes goes bare at home, but keeps in mind Ken's sensitivities. "I usually wear as little as possible when he's there," Kelly says, "but as soon as he leaves, everything comes off! He doesn't care much if I walk around nude, but he doesn't do it, so I don't when he's around."

While Kelly used to belong to a nude club in his area ("It was no big deal to me," he says. "I just couldn't attend enough meetings to be a regular member."), these days he enjoys spending time at the nude beach in his area, and sometimes his partner joins him.

"I just don't think he gets into it as much," Kelly says.

"Besides nude beaches, we've also been to nude guest houses in Key West, and he'll layout nude or go in the pool or hot tub nude. It just seems to be more of a natural way of life for me than it is for him. I just hate wearing clothes."

Half Naked: Interview V

===============

Danny B. and Matt M.
Ft. Lauderdale, FL

Danny B. organized his first nude party when he was 10 years old.

"I convinced my sisters that it would be fun, and we invited a few kids from the neighborhood," Danny remembers. "When I counted to three, everyone disrobed. It was fine until someone knocked over a candle and almost burned down the house," he laughs. "My little sister turned us in to my parents, so I didn't have another party like that until I was an adult living in New York."

As a college student studying theater in the Big Apple, Danny "felt right at home" when he stumbled upon a group of naked men sunbathing on a pier at the end of Christopher Street. He was 18. Despite a very conservative upbringing ("My father wouldn't even let us have breakfast in our pajamas, we had to be fully clothed."), Danny went on to assume leadership roles for New York City's premier nude club, Males au Naturel (MAN)-"I rode nude on the back of a convertible in the Gay Pride parade!" -and for Gay Naturists International (GNI).

Danny's enjoyment of nudism has even spread into his professional life, as well. As an actor, he has appeared nude onstage in many different roles, most recently in the Miami production of "Party," the smash naked comedy that's now enjoying off-Broadway success. Danny currently lives in Ft. Lauderdale with his lover of 1 1/2 years, Matt.

While Danny, who's 33, has been involved with other nudists in the past, his current partner is not a nudist. "I never thought I'd have a relationship with someone who wasn't a nudist," Danny admits.

Danny recounts one of his first dates with Matt: "My company had moved me to Florida. I met Matt at Boots, a Ft. Lauderdale bar with a patio and barbecue. I had just returned from Haulover Beach in Miami and had sand in my shorts. So while my burger was on the grill, I took off my shorts and used the outdoor shower in front of everyone. To me, it was nothing out of the ordinary, but it was shocking to Matt." Still, the couple has been together ever since.

"Matt doesn't see any benefits in the nudist lifestyle," Danny says, "but he has nothing against it. He has never attended a nudist function, and there's nothing I could say or do to persuade him."

Ironically, for a man who has been so active in the naked lifestyle, Danny has chosen to curtail his nude activities to appeal to Matt's sensitivities. "He really doesn't mind if I go to nude parties, but he won't go," Danny says. "And since our schedules are very different, I would rather spend my free time with him. I think it's easier for me to go to the beach and wear my bathing suit than to force him to go to a nude beach."

While Matt, who's 35, has always tolerated Danny's nudist activities ("He even encouraged me to audition for 'Party,'" Danny says.), Danny has tried to woo Matt out of his clothes on many occasions, but to no avail. "One night, I turned off all the lights, put on romantic music and went skinny dipping in the pool under the full moon. When he came home, he went inside and

returned wearing his shorts. I asked him why he didn't want to swim naked, in our own backyard, and he said he was worried about kids in the neighborhood peeking over the fence."

Despite not being as active in the naked lifestyle as he used to be, Danny is still one of its greatest proponents. "To anyone who's never experienced a nude beach or a nude party, I say give it a try! You can always leave if you don't like it."

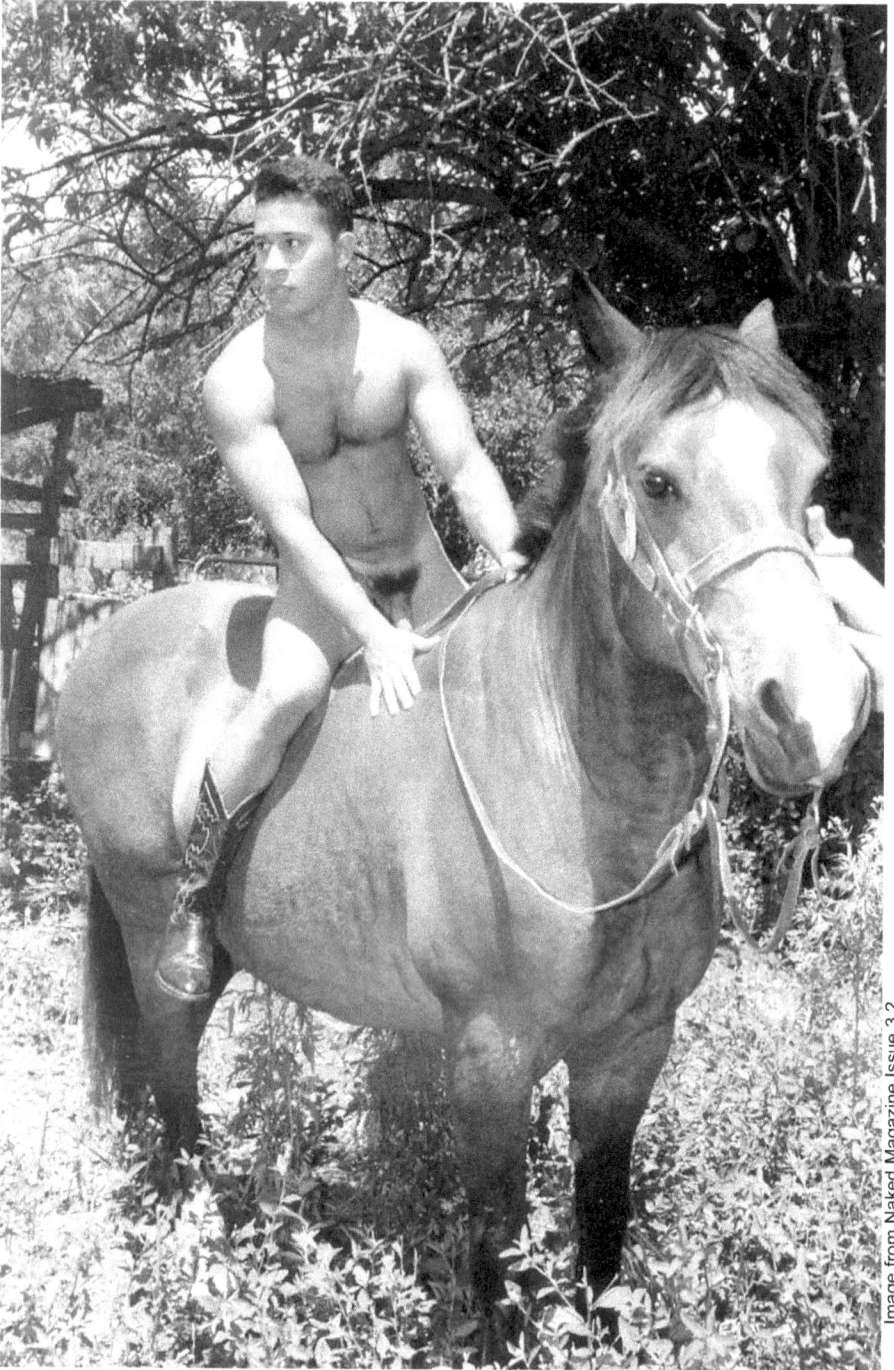

Image from Naked Magazine Issue 3.2

Friendly Ranger Dan

================

I have always enjoyed the freedom of being naked in my home but had never really considered exploring this freedom anywhere else. It was late last July when I took the opportunity to spend a few days camping in the mountainous region of northern Arizona. I hiked about three miles to my favorite campsite, which is right next to a stream, and the clearing is hedged by majestic pines. One feels as if they are the only person in the universe.

As night was approaching, I was relaxing by the campfire when I had the urge to take my clothes off and enjoy the mild evening. It felt incredible! The duality of the sensations of the warmth of the fire and the coolness of the breeze on my naked flesh were nothing short of exhilarating. I lay there for a long time under the starry sky, allowing myself to enjoy the feelings I was experiencing with my naked body before I fell asleep.

The next day I decided to remain naked. This was something new for me and I was loving the feeling of freedom and eroticism that arose. I fished for a long while that morning. I gathered firewood and took a long hike all without my clothes. As I hiked I found myself with an erection that wouldn't go away, and I took time to leisurely jack off. It was intense.

It was about 5 the next evening, as I was preparing to cook my morning's catch, when I heard someone approaching. I was startled and didn't have time to cover myself when a park ranger came into the clearing. I was both embarrassed and aroused by being caught with my pants down. Ranger Dan acted

as if nothing was out of the ordinary. Dan said that he was surprised to find someone in his favorite spot during the middle of
the week. I offered him a beer and we sat talking for quite a
while, him in full uniform and me in full nudity. I invited him to stay
for dinner, which he graciously accepted.

He stepped into the woods to relieve himself as I got busy
cooking dinner. When he returned, he was carrying his uniform
and wearing nothing but a smile! We ate dinner as the sun went
down. After dinner, we just sat there drinking beer and talking.
Being there with attractive naked man was proving to be too
much to handle and I began to get aroused. Without a word spo-
ken by me, he began to stroke himself and I did the same.
Watching this hunky park ranger jack off by the light of the campfire was hot! We both worked our dicks until we came all over
ourselves. We cleaned up and had another beer before Ranger
Dan got dressed and left.

Over the next couple of days I saw a lot of Ranger Dan.
We hiked, fished and talked a lot, but never repeated our campfire experience. I have been camping twice since then and I
can't wait to get out of my clothes, and maybe run into my
favorite park ranger again!

Richard B., Payson, AZ

Factory Frolic

About two years ago, I answered an ad in the local gay paper seeking others who enjoy being naked. The ad was placed by a 35-yearold guy who promptly returned my call.

In the first of several phone calls, I learned that he really enjoyed being naked where he shouldn't, short of risking arrest. He told of shopping for trousers at a major department store and upon seeing himself in his underwear in the dressing room mirror, he got so worked up that he stripped and dared to wander back into the store to grab another pair of pants off the rack.

He began calling me once or twice a month, always around five or six in the evening. He soon revealed that he was calling from work after everyone had left. His lover was considerably uptight about nudism or any sexual activity other than the normal, routine bedroom stuff, so he enjoyed waiting until all the employees were gone from the small container manufacturing business where he worked, and shedding all his clothes to parade naked around the office and factory.

At the time, I was attending monthly meetings of a local nudist club, in which he expressed a great interest. So the calls usually involved me telling him the long and short details of my nudist activities. Though he was hot to attend, his lover's conservatism prevented it. We both enjoyed our talks, especially since he'd explain the physical satisfaction he was getting from hearing all the details of the nudist meetings.

Finally, he began to try to talk me into coming to his factory for a mutual naked romp around the machines. While I've always felt totally comfortable being naked around others, it's always in a setting where I could relax, knowing I wasn't flirting with arrest or confronting others who might become offended by my nudity. So it was quite a hard sell for going into a strange business where I'd be relying totally on my yet unseen friend's word that nobody would be returning unexpectedly.

But I finally gave in. It was a very hot summer afternoon, a Friday. My friend promised that no regular employee would be back before Monday and that the two managers, the only ones who could potentially surprise us, were out of town together on business. We'd be completely alone. And perfectly safe.

The voice on the phone soon turned out to be a hot little hunk! About 5-foot-7, slim torso, with a moderate display of muscles all around. Black hair outlined his chest perfectly. His short cropped hair and closely trimmed full beard added to a butch little package with a very generous endowment. Just as nice and horny as you could get!

So there we were, totally naked, strolling around his office and out into the factory, climbing around and posing on various machines. It would have made a hot video for my own personal library! He'd brought a porn tape to play on the office VCR for a little inspiration between our rounds in the factory, not that I really needed any help!

To get even more exposure for our naked bodies, he opened two large sliding doors across one whole end of the small warehouse building. What a video scene that would have made! Wearing only hiking boots, he leaned hard into pushing open each door, showing off each and every muscle, from arms and shoulders down his back to his fuzzy butt and legs. There we stood, swinging free in the breeze, facing several other, now empty, neighboring businesses.

Needless to say, our naked romp, which lasted about two hours, had a voluminous conclusion, no doubt spurred on by the edge of uncertainty: would we be seen?

To my great disappointment, that was the last I saw or heard of my enterprising little workplace nudist. I just hope that wherever he is, he's still naked!

Bill, Dallas, TX

Image from Naked Magazine Issue 2.4

Hawaiian Camping Buddy

===============

I have always had the desire to go naked in public, but I know the problems this could cause due to public attitudes. My opinion is that we were all brought into this world naked, so why shouldn't we be allowed to stay naked throughout our lives? I'm holding out the hope that someday we'll be able to realize that dream!

The closest I ever came to a total nude lifestyle was living in Hawaii from 1973-1978. While there, I did a lot of hiking in the tropical wilderness. I had a favorite trail I used often. After I had hiked about two miles, I would take off my shirt and shorts and continue hiking in only my boots. This was very exciting to me, to feel the cool breeze blowing all over my body. I had an exclusive camping site I used back in the mountains which was my usual destination.

One such time, I thought I spotted someone about a quarter-mile behind me but I did not let that interfere with my desire to continue hiking. After stripping down to just my hiking boots, I put on my backpack and continued my hike to the campsite. Once there, I proceeded to set up camp for the night.

About an hour later, someone called to me from the trails, asking if he could come into my camp, and I said okay. This guy came in through the bushes and I think he was a little surprised to see me standing there naked, but he didn't seem bothered by it at all.

He said his name was James, and he began set up his

tent across from mine, disappearing inside to stow his pack and spread out his sleeping bag. When he emerged from the tent, to my delight he was naked, too!

We had a great time that weekend. There was no sex, we just kicked back and enjoyed being out in the wilderness without any clothes on. We later developed a friendship that lasted more than five years. James was in the military and had to relocate to a new area - I miss my naked camping buddy very much!

Fred G., Ft. Lauderdale, FL

Signing for the Package

=================

I don't know where you get your stories from but here is an experience that happened to me a couple of years ago.

It was during the summer, I was taking my usual late Saturday morning shower when the front doorbell rang. I quickly finished rinsing off and grabbed a towel, and as I was running to the door, wrapped it around my hips. I opened the door while still dripping to find that a very young mailman had a package for me that I needed to sign for. Since I was wearing just a towel, he decided it was easier for him to step into the doorway, rather than have me come out onto the stoop.

He handed me his clipboard for me to sign on the proper line, and as we were exchanging the clipboard and the package, my towel fell onto the floor, leaving me there with just a panicked expression on my face! I was fumbling between the package and the clipboard and didn't know what to grab first! He came to my rescue by dropping to the floor to pick up the towel. He was as shocked as I was and was fumbling around. It took him four tries before he finally got the towel back around my hips! He must have bumped into my dick at least half a dozen times as he was trying to get the towel around me, which started to bring it to attention. Thank God he was as quick as he was or it would soon have sprung up and poked him in the eye!

I handed him back his clipboard and told him I was sorry; and that I didn't mean to embarrass him, and that this had never happened to me before. He smiled and told me that he wasn't offended or embarrassed and not to worry about it. He told me to have a great day and started down the stoop. He then looked over his shoulder and gave me a wink and kept on walking.

I never saw him again, and later found out that he and his cute bubble butt were just filling in that day for my regular carrier. I wouldn't mind losing the towel again someday; especially if I was able to get him to strip at the same time!

John J., Long Island, NY

Ready for their Close-ups!

==================

A couple of years ago, three guys I knew and I decided to go on a hike up in the Cascades. The three of us knew each other from high school but were not good friends. We all liked hiking and had talked about going on a hike for several months.

It was a nice May Saturday-sunny, temperature in the mid-60s, and clear skies. Mike, Terry, Alan and I (Dan) drove into the mountains and parked at a camping area. We had hiking boots, our clothes, and gear, including water and snacks. We left the parking lot on foot and hiked into the woods.

After walking about an hour or so we got to a clearing by a small stream. We hadn't seen anyone thus far during our hike. We decided to take a break so we sat by the stream. Soon, a couple of guys came by and the six of us started talking about hiking and other things. The conversation turned to nudism and these two guys (whose names were Jeff and Pat) were talking about how they sometimes went hiking naked and how they sometimes videotaped each other nude in the woods.

Pat took out a camcorder from their pack and said that they were planning on taping each other that day. Jeff asked us what we thought about that and if we would like to be videotaped. Terry seemed to be turned on to the idea and Mike was against it. Alan and I were kind of neutral. Pat asked us if he and Jeff could tape us. Mike flatly said no, and Terry said he was for it. I asked them what we would get out of it and they offered to pay us for an hour or so of filming.

Terry, Alan, Mike and I went off by ourselves to talk about it. Terry was for it and I said it sounded good-we could all use some extra pocket money. Alan agreed but it was hard to convince Mike. We finally talked Mike into it after about five minutes and then went back to where Jeff and Pat were waiting and told them okay, as long as the money was up front. We went over some things about the filming before we started.

First Jeff and Pat got the tape out, loaded the camera, and scouted out the right locations. Then Terry, Alan, Mike and I stripped off our shirts. At the time I had an average build with some muscles from lifting at the gym, dark brown hair and some hair on my chest. Terry also had an average build, black hair and a hairy chest with small, thick nipples that jutted out. Alan took off his shirt to reveal a slender body, his chest, arms and legs were covered with blond fur. Mike was a smooth redhead, with a medium build and had large, thick nipples.

After getting filmed with our shirts off, it was time to take our pants off. Terry was wearing blue briefs; Alan had on a pair of baggy striped boxers; Mike and I wore jockstraps. I wondered what my buddies' packages would look like and I soon found out!

Pat told us it was time to peel off our remaining clothes. I took off my jock to show my average set. Terry peeled off his briefs to reveal another average set but his dick was uncut and had a lot of skin covering the tip. Alan went third, dropping his boxers to show us his package-average dick with big balls all partly hidden by a thick blond bush. Mike finally peeled off his jock. He had a small package with a thick red-orange bush.

Jeff filmed us as a group then individually, both front and back. Then Pat said to just walk around the clearing so Jeff could film us in action. I noticed that Terry's skin was pulling back off his dick a little and thought that he was getting turned on to this scene. I was getting turned on to Mike's cute body. Mike was the shyest of our group-maybe because of his small package. Alan walked around the clearing, his big balls swaying back and forth as he moved, glancing at our packages.

Pat wanted us to do some exercises next while Jeff filmed us, so we lined up in a row. First, we did a few push-ups while Jeff filmed us from the rear. Jeff then got back in front of us and we did deep knee bends with our legs spread apart. After that we did a bunch of jumping jacks. I was mesmerized by watching Alan's balls flopping up and down with each jump!

Terry was getting real turned on by this and his skin had pulled back completely, showing a reddish cock head. His dick was about half hard. So was mine. Alan's was pointing out, away from his body and his heavy swinging balls. It seemed that even Mike was getting into this somewhat since his cute stub dick was hard and sticking out from the forest of red-orange hair.

Pat had us walk along the stream bank a ways while Jeff filmed our backs and butts. Then we turned around and walked back so Jeff could film our front sides. After that, we got into the stream, which was very shallow, and played around somewhat with each other-splashing water, grabbing arms, fake punches, etc. This went on for over an hour and we finally told Pat and Jeff that it was enough. Jeff finished up his filming as we got out of the stream. The two of them thanked us, said they hoped to see us again someday, and left. We sat around, still naked, and talked about the experience we just had.

The four of us have gotten together several more times for hikes but we haven't gone hiking naked since, and we've not seen Pat or Jeff again.

Dan, Auburn, WA

Image from Naked Magazine Issue 3.2

Motorcycle Ride

===============

It was one of those rare summer days in Northern California when it was hot, even at the beach. I rode my motorcycle to a nude beach popular with gays, and spent a wonderful day there just frolicking and soaking up sunshine. Even the 55 degree ocean water was inviting, and as the waves splashed against my naked dick, I felt it get hard, then soft again, repeatedly.

Finally, it came time to leave. It was still hot, so I rode shirtless, wearing only a pair of running shorts and a helmet. The highway I took is famous among motorcyclists for its smooth, gently winding road with few cars and even fewer cops, and I was enjoying the sun on my back and the warm wind on my skin. The wind found its way into the leg opening of my shorts, and I felt it caressing and cooling my sweaty dick and balls.

After spending the day at the nude beach, I was unwilling to give up any more nakedness than necessary. I pulled up the sides of my shorts as far as they would go. It occurred to me that in my riding position, my crotch could not be seen either from ahead, where it was blocked by the gas tank, or from behind. Emboldened, I widened the opening in my shorts and let the wind reach my crotch with greater force.

My dick responded to this increased stimulation by growing, and soon extended out of the leg opening. The thought that passing motorists could now see (if they were looking at the right spot at the instant they zoomed by) got me even more excited. I pulled my dick and balls completely out of my shorts.

The full force of the wind and occasional splashes of sun, on my dick soon had it at full attention. With my left hand, I began to caress it. Here I was, beating off on a public highway, fully exposed to the occasional car zooming by. I felt an enormous sense of freedom, which added to the pleasure I was feeling all over my body. What a beautiful world it would be, I thought, when the glory of the exposed human body and its natural erotic functions, are accepted wherever they are found.

I continued this way for about 10 miles, rubbing the precum off on the motorcycle's tank. I didn't cum; having an orgasm while operating a motorcycle at high speed is definitely something I'd consider "unsafe sex"! As I approached town, I stuffed my now deflating cock back into my shorts, where it continued to receive the cooling wind, although now hidden from sight. By the time I got home, I was left with a warm feeling and an exciting memory. I can't wait for another hot day at the beach! Maybe the shorts will come entirely off next time!

C.L., Santa Clara, CA

Rest Stop Discovery

=================

It was a nice evening in late August and I was sitting on the porch totally nude with just a towel around me. I decided to call a friend to see if he wanted to cruise around. He did, so we rode around town naked and every so often we would get out so people could see us. We rode around for awhile and had some fun and after dropping him off, I decided I wasn't quite ready to end my adventure and go home.

I decided to ride down to the Interstate and, after drinking a can of soda, had to use the restroom. By this time, it was around two in the morning. I parked at the rest area and looked around. I said to myself, "Why put any clothes on? Just walk to the restroom naked!" I looked around and got the nerve to get out of my car and walk to the building.

It was such a rush! My nervousness was gone and the idea of doing this suddenly felt great! To my surprise, when I was walking back to the car, I saw two guys corning in to the restroom. They had on shorts and T-shirts. One guy looked at me and said to his buddy, "I can't believe that guy!" I didn't say anything since I was totally naked and I didn't know how they would react. I was a little nervous of what could possibly happen, but since I'm an exhibitionist, I was really getting a charge out of it!

The two guys came out and got back in their van. I could see them looking out the windows, trying to get a glimpse of me in my car. I told myself, "Get back out again," and I did, and walked down the sidewalk to where the van was parked. There were only about five other cars in the lot, and from what I could tell everyone in them was asleep. Of course, the two guys started up their van and backed down to around a couple of spaces from where I was standing. Not sure what they were up to, I turned around and hurried back to my car.

The van just sat there, though, and waited for another car to pull in and then leave. The driver opened his door after the car pulled away. The guy got out of the van totally naked! His passenger opened his door and stepped out and he was totally naked, also! They walked past my car and let me see everything they had to offer. After talking to them for a little while, I discovered they also are nudists, and often walk around naked in public, but had never met anyone to hang out with. They said finding someone else into public nudity was a "real thrill" for them. We three get together and hang out naked at least once a week, sometimes pushing the envelope in public places. Hopefully one of our future adventures will bring us face to face with others who are also into this scene.

Gary, Lexington, KY

Family Reunion Afterglow

===============

I've never written a story to your magazine before. I hope your readers like this adventure that happened to me!

It was the end of August, around 2 in the morning. I was just returning from my family reunion in New Jersey. I was almost home, about a half-mile from my house, when I passed a light blue Lincoln Town Car on the side of the road. There was a young, well-built and hung naked man standing in front of the headlights, taking a piss. I made a U-turn right there and came back to him. He walked over to my car and told me to come get naked with him. I never had done anything like that before, but I did as he asked.

Now there we were on the side of a public highway totally naked and I just knew a state trooper would pull by at any minute and throw both of us in jail. The excitement of it all, however, was worth it!

This beautiful man started to rub his hands all over my body, filling me with even more excitement than I already was feeling. I started rubbing him in return and both of us became so hard it wasn't funny. He led me to the hood of his car. We spent the next 20 minutes on the hood of his 1996 Lincoln posing nude for each other and finally making love. We did everything imaginable to each other. We kept pulling back so we could climax together, and finally couldn't take it any longer and blew our loads all over the hood of the car. After that we gave each other a long kiss and bid farewell. I got in my car and drove home the rest of the way totally naked.

I live in a mobile home park and you can imagine how close together the units are. But I couldn't bother getting dressed, so I walked from my car back to my front door, unlocked it and went right to bed, completely nude.

Every night now, as soon as I get home from work, the clothes come off and I stay naked until it's time to go back the work the following day. I even take rides in my car naked, hoping to see if my Town Car stud is back on the side of the road again. I haven't seen him again, but I have a good feeling that I will!

Harry B., Laurel, DE

NAKED
MAGAZINE
REAL STORIES
FIRST EDITION
VOLUMES 1.1 - 2.1
ENCOUNTERS AND ADVENTURES

More Titles at:
www.GoodBoner.com

NAKED MAGAZINE

SECOND EDITION
VOLUMES 2.2-3.1

REAL STORIES

ENCOUNTERS AND ADVENTURES

More Titles at:
www.GoodBoner.com

Naked Magazine